Contents

Baking Soda Basics

Put over 160 years of versatility and value to work throughout your home.

Now, the cleaning and freshening secret that has been passed down for generations is yours. There's almost nothing ARM & HAMMER® Baking Soda can't do. You can trust its natural, pure, and gentle power to tackle jobs in every room of your home— and beyond!

ARM & HAMMER® Baking Soda is strong enough to lift away dirt, but still gentle and non-abrasive on delicate surfaces. And when it comes to odors, ARM & HAMMER® Baking Soda

America's #1 Trusted Baking Soda Brand

Household Uses for
Baking Soda

Over 100
Helpful Solutions & Tips

ARM & HAMMER

THE STANDARD OF PURITY ®

One Box, Countless Uses.

pil

Publications International, Ltd.

Publications
International, Ltd.

neutralizes and eliminates them at the source.

Try these effective, money-saving solutions and make the secret of ARM & HAMMER® Baking Soda yours today!

Baking Soda Basics

The tips you'll find in this book use ARM & HAMMER® Baking Soda in four different ways: Directly, in a solution, as a paste, and as an additive. Follow these guidelines for each use when a specific measurement isn't given. For added convenience, ARM & HAMMER® Baking Soda is available in an array of sizes and forms, making choosing the right product for any job easy.

1. Use Directly
Baking Soda is sprinkled directly on the surface or onto a sponge for use. It is not diluted.

2. Make a Solution
Use 4 tablespoons of Baking Soda for each quart of warm water.

3. Make a Paste
Add just enough water to the Baking Soda to achieve a consistency that will not run if applied to a vertical surface.

4. As an Additive
Follow the directions for each tip, adding the appropriate amount of Baking Soda to improve the cleaning and deodorizing performance of products you already use in your home.

Chapter 1

Personal Care

When you're making time to take care of you, ARM & HAMMER® Baking Soda has easy and affordable ways to help you refresh and relax. Baking Soda is the simple, all-natural secret to glowing skin; softer, more manageable hair; fresher breath; and so much more.

Refreshing Bath Soak

Taking a bath is so last year…until now! Add ½ cup of ARM & HAMMER® Baking Soda to your bath for a relaxing and refreshing soak. Your skin will feel silky smooth, and it's a great way to get away from it all.

Brightening Manicure

Dip brush into ARM & HAMMER® Baking Soda and scrub nails and cuticles. Make a paste of 3 parts ARM & HAMMER® Baking Soda to 1 part water. Rub in a gentle, circular motion over hands and fingers to exfoliate and smooth. Rinse clean with warm water and apply polish as usual.

Brushes and Combs

For lustrous hair with more shine, keep brushes and combs clean. Remove natural oil build-up and hair product residue by soaking combs and brushes in a solution of 1 teaspoon of ARM & HAMMER® Baking Soda in a small basin of warm water. Rinse and allow to dry.

Antacid

Spicy food is yummy until it bothers the tummy. ARM & HAMMER® Baking Soda is a safe and effective antacid to relieve heartburn, sour stomach, and/or acid  indigestion, when used as directed. Always refer to the ARM & HAMMER® Baking Soda package for instructions.*

Directions:
Add ½ teaspoon to ½ glass (4 ounces) of water every 2 hours, or as directed by a physician. Dissolve completely in water. Accurately measure ½ teaspoon.**

*Warnings:
• Ask a doctor before use if you have a sodium restricted diet.
• Ask a doctor or a pharmacist before use if you are taking a prescription drug. Antacids may interact with certain prescription drugs.
• Do not administer to children under age 5.
• STOMACH WARNING: TO AVOID SERIOUS INJURY, DO NOT TAKE UNTIL POWDER IS COMPLETELY DISSOLVED. IT IS VERY IMPORTANT NOT TO TAKE THIS PRODUCT WHEN OVERLY FULL FROM FOOD OR DRINK. Consult a doctor if severe stomach pain occurs after taking this product.
• Stop use and ask a doctor if symptoms last more than 2 weeks.
**Do not take more than the following amounts in 24 hours:
  • Seven ½ teaspoons
  • Three ½ teaspoons if you are over 60 years.
    Do not use the maximum dosage for more than 2 weeks.

Other Information:
Each ½ teaspoon contains 616 g sodium.
Refer to the ARM & HAMMER® Baking Soda package for detailed instructions before using.

Hand Cleanser

Give yourself a hand with ARM & HAMMER® Baking Soda. Forget the harsh soaps and gently scrub away ground-in dirt and neutralize odors on hands with a paste of 3 parts ARM & HAMMER® Baking Soda to 1 part water, or add 3 parts ARM & HAMMER® Baking Soda to your liquid hand soap. Then rinse clean. Your skin will feel softer too!

Mouth Freshening

Bad breath keeping you tight-lipped? Open up for ARM & HAMMER® Baking Soda. Put 1 teaspoon in half a glass of water, swish, spit, and rinse. (Avoid swallowing excess rinse solution.) Odors are neutralized—not just covered up—so get ready to pucker up!

Foot Soak

Here's a great way to start your home pedicure. Dissolve 3 tablespoons of ARM & HAMMER® Baking Soda in a basin of warm water and soak feet. Gently scrub with a paste of ARM & HAMMER® Baking Soda. The hardest part is deciding which color nail polish you'll use this week!

Mouth Cleansing

Clean up your mouth! Use ARM & HAMMER®
Baking Soda to help keep teeth clean and
white! Sprinkle some ARM & HAMMER®
Baking Soda in a small dish, dip in your
damp toothbrush, brush, and rinse throroughly
to freshen those pearly whites.*

*ARM & HAMMER® Baking Soda does not contain the
anti-cavity ingredient fluoride. Use it where water is
fluorinated or when a non-fluoride toothpaste is desired for
adult use or as directed by your dentist or physician.*

Hair Care

For locks that
rock, remember to
shake it. Sprinkle
a small amount
(quarter-size) of
ARM & HAMMER®
Baking Soda into
your palm along
with your favorite shampoo.
Shampoo as usual and rinse
thoroughly. (Be careful to avoid
eye area when rinsing.) The
ARM & HAMMER® Baking Soda
helps remove the residue that
styling products leave behind so
your hair is cleaner and more
manageable.

Smelly Sneakers

Smelly sneakers are embarrassing and completely preventable. Simply shake a little ARM & HAMMER® Baking Soda into them between wearings. It works by absorbing odor-causing moisture while neutralizing existing odors. Use at least once a week or more if you wear the shoes frequently. Tap out excess Baking Soda before wearing your sneakers again.

Oral Appliance Soak

Soak oral appliances like retainers, mouthpieces, and dentures in a solution of 2 teaspoons ARM & HAMMER® Baking Soda dissolved in a glass or small bowl of warm water. Then rinse throroughly. The ARM & HAMMER® Baking Soda loosens food particles and neutralizes odors to keep appliances fresh! You can also brush appliances clean using ARM & HAMMER® Baking Soda.

Plaque

Tooth decay may result from food debris that leads to plaque build-up. ARM & HAMMER® toothpastes, with the power of Baking Soda, penetrate deep down into the crevices between your teeth and gums to remove plaque in hard-to-reach places.

Deodorant

A quick pit stop. Dust ARM & HAMMER® Baking Soda under arms as needed to feel fresh all day. The magic of ARM & HAMMER® Baking Soda naturally absorbs odors instead of just covering them up.

Bug Bites Be Gone

Baking Soda temporarily protects and helps relieve minor skin irritation and itching due to insect bites. Refer to the ARM & HAMMER® Baking Soda package for detailed instructions before using.*

Facial and Body Exfoliator

Are you a fan of the self-tan? Before applying products that give you a glow, give yourself an invigorating, yet gentle, facial and body scrub with ARM & HAMMER® Baking Soda. Removing dead skin cells will leave your skin soft and smooth, perfect before application. Make a paste of 3 parts ARM & HAMMER® Baking Soda to 1 part water. Rub in a gentle circular motion to exfoliate the skin. Rinse clean, being careful to avoid eye area.

Shaving

Men with sensitive skin
may find that a solution of
1 tablespoon ARM & HAMMER® Baking Soda in
1 cup water makes a great preshave treatment or a
soothing aftershave treatment. Avoid eye area.

Razor Burn

For instant relief of razor burn, dab on an
ARM & HAMMER® Baking Soda solution.

Sunburn Pain

For sunburn pain, saturate a washcloth with a solution of
4 tablespoons ARM & HAMMER® Baking Soda in
1 quart water. Apply to affected area.

Poison Ivy, Oak, and Sumac Irritation

Ease irritation from poison ivy, oak, and sumac. Refer
to the ARM & HAMMER® Baking Soda package
for detailed instructions before using.*

*Warnings:
• When using this product, do not get into eyes.
• In some cases, soaking too long may overdry.
• Stop use and ask a doctor if conditions worsen or symptoms last more
than 7 days or clear up and occur again within a few days.

Directions:
For adults and children 2 years of age and older, children under 2 years
ask a doctor.

For a paste: add enough water to the Baking Soda to form paste. Apply
to the affected area of skin as needed or as directed by a doctor.

For a soak in the bath: dissolve 1 to 2 cups in a tub of warm water. Soak
for 10 to 30 minutes or as directed by doctor. Pat dry (do not rub) to
keep a thin layer on the skin.

For use as a compress or wet dressing: add Baking Soda to water to
make a mixture in a container. Soak a clean, wet cloth in the mixture.
Apply cloth loosely to affected area for 15 to 30 minutes. Repeat as
needed or directed by a doctor. Discard mixture after each use.

Chapter 2

Baby & Nursery Care

We have a special place in our hearts and a long history of caring for families, and lots of ways to help! All-natural ARM & HAMMER® Baking Soda is a pure and gentle choice to safely clean and freshen baby's home environment. From deodorizing baby bottles to neutralizing diaper odors, trust ARM & HAMMER®.

Freshen Stuffed Animals

Even Mr. Bear needs a freshening. Keep favorite cuddly toys fresh with a dry shower of ARM & HAMMER® Baking Soda. Just sprinkle ARM & HAMMER® Baking Soda on dry toys and let it sit for 15 minutes before thoroughly brushing off to remove residue. It's gentle enough for use around your baby and Teddy will appreciate it too!

Deodorize Baby Bottles

Do you know what goes in your baby's mouth? For safe cleaning and deodorizing, fill bottles with warm water and add 1 teaspoon of ARM & HAMMER® Baking Soda. Shake, rinse, and thoroughly clean as usual. For extra cleaning and deodorizing, you can also soak bottles and nipples overnight in a solution of 4 tablespoons of ARM & HAMMER® Baking Soda to 1 quart of warm water. Then rinse and clean as usual.

Cleaning Baby Equipment

Little hands mean lots of exploring. Safely clean your
baby's area (play pen, changing table, crib, stroller, car
seat, and high chair) with ARM & HAMMER® Baking
Soda. Just sprinkle ARM & HAMMER® Baking Soda
directly on a clean, damp sponge and rub the item clean.
Wipe down thoroughly and allow to dry. Sparkling clean
and no harsh cleaners to worry about!

Baby Spills on Carpet

Even little ones can make big messes! Clean and deodorize baby spills or accidents on carpets by soaking up as much of the spill as possible. Clean the stain according to the carpet manufacturer's directions and allow to dry. Then, to deodorize, when the area is completely dry, sprinkle liberally with ARM & HAMMER® Baking Soda and let sit for 15 minutes before vacuuming it up. Check for color-fastness first before applying ARM & HAMMER® Baking Soda.*

Deodorize Diaper Pails

Whoa! A smell this powerful needs to be neutralized. Sprinkle ARM & HAMMER® Baking Soda liberally over dirty disposable diapers in the diaper pail.

Make Bath Water Soothing

Add ¼ cup of ARM & HAMMER® Baking Soda to a regular tub, or a few tablespoons to a baby tub, with warm water for a soothing soak for baby's bottom and skin.

*CAUTION: Before use, test hidden area of carpet for color-fastness. Mix ½ tablespoon in ½ cup water and pour small amount on carpet. Let dry, vacuum, and check carpet.

Baby Laundry

ARM & HAMMER® Baking Soda is gentle enough for even the tiniest baby clothes, yet effective enough for big baby odors. For tough stains, add ½ cup of ARM & HAMMER® Baking Soda with your liquid laundry detergent, or a ½ cup in the rinse cycle for deodorization!

Clean Baby Combs

Harsh chemicals are
a hair-raising thought.
Keep baby combs and
brushes clean by soaking
them in gentle solution of 1 teaspoon
of ARM & HAMMER® Baking Soda in a small
basin of warm water. Rinse and allow to dry.

Cleaning Baby Toys

Don't toy around with harsh cleaners. Clean and
deodorize baby toys safely and effectively using
4 tablespoons of ARM & HAMMER® Baking Soda
dissolved in 1 quart of warm water. Wash toys with
a clean, damp sponge or cloth, rinse, and dry.

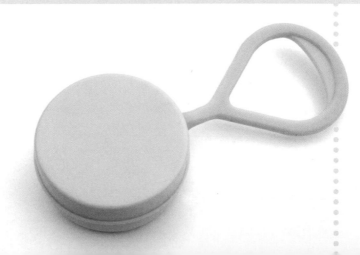

Chapter 3

Fun
for Kids

Who doesn't love easy and fun
ideas to entertain kids and help
them learn, all for about a dollar
a solution? ARM & HAMMER® can
help with great Baking Soda
projects and crafts, like safe,
non-toxic Play Clay™ and
our famous Erupting
Volcano. We
have great
ways to play!

Water Colors

Have an urge to create? These paints mix up in minutes with items you have in your kitchen! Experiment to get the most vibrant colors for your masterpiece. (Do not eat or drink the watercolors. Children should use only under adult supervision.)

WHAT YOU NEED:
- 2 tablespoons ARM & HAMMER® Baking Soda
- 2 tablespoons flour
- 2 teaspoons sugar
- 1 packet* dry unsweetened drink mix (any flavor)
- 2 tablespoons water

HOW TO MAKE IT:
1. Mix dry ingredients in a bowl.
2. Add water and stir until fizzing stops. (Different flavors of the drink mix will yield different colors.)
3. For more intense watercolor, a few drops of food coloring can be added to the mix.
4. Paint with them right away, or pour into jars with lids and try to let harden for future use.

*Packets vary in size, depending on flavor. Use enough drink mix to make 2 quarts. Remember the importance of adult supervision, especially with young children.

Sneaker Peekers

This fun craft does double duty. Kids will have a blast decorating these zany creatures—and then the ARM & HAMMER® Baking Soda will go to work deodorizing those smelly sneakers!

WHAT YOU NEED:
- Newspaper
- 1 new, white athletic sock (mid-calf size)
- 1 cup ARM & HAMMER® Baking Soda
- 1 rubber band
- 6-inch ribbon or string
- Felt, markers, buttons, and glue for decorating!

HOW TO MAKE IT:

1. Lay newspaper down on your work surface.

2. Fill the sock with 1 cup ARM & HAMMER® Baking Soda.

3. Secure with rubber band.

4. Tie ribbon around rubber band, cut off extra sock (cuff area).

5. Decorate! Use felt, markers, buttons, sequins, etc. to make your sneaker peeker an animal, a monster, or a flower! Anything goes!

6. Double the supplies to make two peekers to stick in your sneakers overnight for fresh shoes in the morning! (Remember the importance of adult supervision, especially with young children.)

Erupting Volcano

This is an old favorite that's a staple at science fairs. (Be sure to supervise young children.)

WHAT YOU NEED:
- Cardboard
- 3 (4 ounce) plastic cups
- Plaster-of-Paris
- ¼ cup vinegar
- Few drops of hand dishwashing liquid
- Few drops of water
- Few drops of red food coloring
- 1 teaspoon ARM & HAMMER® Baking Soda

HOW TO MAKE IT:
1. On baking sheet (or other easily cleaned surface), shape cardboard into broad cone shape using a cup to form a "crater" at the top of the volcano.
2. Use Plaster-of-Paris over the cone to form the volcano (do not get plaster into the crater). Allow volcano to dry completely.
3. Paint or decorate volcano as desired.
4. Mix vinegar with dishwashing liquid, water, and red food coloring in a plastic cup.
5. Put ARM & HAMMER® Baking Soda into a small, empty plastic cup. Place this cup inside the volcano crater.
6. Quickly pour vinegar mixture into the ARM & HAMMER® Baking Soda cup in the crater. Enjoy the "lava" as the volcano erupts!

EXPLANATION:
The ARM & HAMMER® Baking Soda reacts with the vinegar in the mixture and produces a gas: carbon dioxide (CO_2). The gas releases bubbles through the dishwashing liquid and food coloring, creating the bubbly, red lava.

Cork Races

Use the reaction between ARM & HAMMER® Baking Soda and vinegar to create a racing game!

WHAT YOU NEED:
- Tape
- Several lengths of clear plastic tubing (1 inch inner diameter, each approximately 3 feet in length)
- 1 tablespoon ARM & HAMMER® Baking Soda
- Painted cork balls (¾ inch diameter or small enough to pass easily through tubing)
- ½ cup vinegar
- Hand dishwashing liquid
- Small container with spout

HOW TO MAKE IT:
1. Tape up 1 end of each tube to be the bottom.
2. Stand tubes upright on a flat surface (baking sheet or tray) and pour ARM & HAMMER® Baking Soda into the bottom.
3. Drop a cork ball into each tube.
4. Make a mixture of vinegar and dishwashing liquid in the spouted container.
5. Pour the mix carefully down the inside of the tube and watch the cork ride the suds to the top. Keep face away from top of tube to avoid being splashed. (Supervise use with young children.)

EXPLANATION:
The Baking Soda reacts with the vinegar in the mixture and produces a gas: carbon dioxide (CO_2). As the gas

is released it bubbles through the dishwashing liquid, creating the suds that push the cork to the top.

VARIATIONS:

- Experiment with different mixes of vinegar, ARM & HAMMER® Baking Soda, and dishwashing liquid and have races to find the mix that makes the fastest cork.

- Mark the tubes ⅔ of the way to the top. Experiment with mixes and quantities to get the cork to stop closest to the mark.

- Try ping-pong balls instead of cork balls and use wider-diameter tubing.

Footprints

Let the kids have some holiday fun while you clean and eliminate odors! Sprinkle some ARM & HAMMER® Baking Soda in a stencil to leave Santa footprints on the rug. When the kids are done playing (or after 15 minutes), vacuum the Baking Soda to freshen carpets.*

*CAUTION: Before use, test hidden area of carpet for color-fastness. Mix ½ tablespoon in ½ cup water and pour small amount on carpet. Let dry, vacuum, and check carpet.

Play Clay™

Play Clay™ is homemade modeling clay that hardens after drying. Three simple ingredients combine for virtually unlimited creative possibilities for kids of all ages. Play Clay™ is great for rainy days, birthday parties, and class activities. Use it to make decorations, ornaments, jewelry, magnets, boxes, and more!

WHAT YOU NEED:
• 2 cups ARM & HAMMER® Baking Soda
• 1 cup cornstarch
• 1¼ cups cold water (can add food coloring to color clay)

HOW TO MAKE IT:
1. Stir together ARM & HAMMER® Baking Soda and cornstarch in saucepan.

2. Add water (and food coloring, if desired) and cook over medium heat, stirring constantly, until mixture reaches consistency of moist mashed potatoes (approximately 10 to 15 minutes).
3. Remove mixture to plate and cover with a damp cloth.

When Play Clay™ is cool to the touch, pat until smooth. Now you're ready to make fun shapes! (Do not eat clay. Children should use with adult supervision.) Once done playing, air dry clay shapes on a wire rack (8 hours or overnight). Or, preheat oven to lowest setting. Turn off, then place finished shapes on a cookie sheet in oven for 10 to 15 minutes. Decorate with paint, markers, or glitter, or add your favorite objects (like buttons and shells) with a small amount of glue. Store any unused Play Clay™ in the refrigerator for up to 1 week (store in a tightly sealed plastic bag or container). Do not freeze.

Play Clay™ Hanger
Capture a child's handprint in Play Clay™ by pressing into damp clay. When dry, paint and add the child's name and date on back, then attach a picture hanger.

Play Clay™ Frame
Cut a square or rectangle from Play Clay™ then cut a frame opening the size of a favorite photograph. Leave a ½-inch border. Use another piece of clay for a stand to attach to the back. Decorate the frame.

Play Clay™ Plaques

Create a name plaque for a child's room by cutting out the shapes of letters and attaching them to a rectangular piece of Play Clay™ as the background. Paint and finish when dry.

Play Clay™ Jewelry

Shape beads for a necklace by rolling Play Clay™ into oval or round shapes. Press a toothpick through to make holes for stringing.

Play Clay™ Threading

String Play Clay™ beads on thread, shoelaces, yarn, kite string, or fishing line. Tie knots between beads to hold them in place.

Play Clay™ Earrings

To make earrings or a brooch, create small shapes with a flat backside and glue to earrings or pin backings.

Play Clay™ Napkin Rings

Make fancy napkin rings by rolling out a long, narrow rectangle of clay, then piecing the ends together into a ring.

Play Clay™ Ornaments

Use cookie cutters to make tree ornaments. While the ornament is still wet, make a hole near the top for hanging. Add an ornament hook or ribbon to hang the ornament.

Play Clay™ Paintings

Paint dry pieces with watercolor, poster, or acrylic paints. Draw with a felt-tip pen or waterproof marker. Apply glitter to wet paint.

Tips for Working with Play Clay™

1. Smooth rough or cracked edges of Play Clay™ with an emery board.
2. Finish Play Clay™ objects with a clear acrylic spray or clear nail polish.

Inflate a Balloon

Remove the cap sealing ring from an empty 2-liter soda bottle. Pour 1 cup of vinegar into the bottle. Prestretch your balloon and fill with 2 tablespoons of ARM & HAMMER® Baking Soda. Close the neck of the balloon with a bobby pin, leaving enough room at the end of the balloon to stretch over the bottle's neck. Carefully place balloon over neck of bottle and down about ¾ of an inch so the ring of the balloon is sealed around the neck. Remove the bobby pin and invert the balloon to dispense Baking Soda into the bottle. To remove: gently raise the edge of the balloon to allow the gas to escape in a direction away from you.

Chapter 4

Cleaning & Freshening Homes with Pets

Pets bring lots of love into a home, but you don't have to live with their odors! You can use the power of ARM & HAMMER® Baking Soda to eliminate even the toughest pet odors, from litter boxes to carpets and upholstery and more.

Dirty Dog

Use ARM & HAMMER® Baking Soda to give your dog a dry bath. Start when your dog's coat is thoroughly dry. Give fur a light sprinkle of ARM & HAMMER® Baking Soda, use a brush to work it through, and then thoroughly remove. It's an easy way to freshen your best friend's coat in between baths.

Cat Litter Deodorizer

Cat got your nose? ARM & HAMMER® Baking Soda freshens your cat's litter box for oh so 'pawfect' freshness. Cover the bottom of the pan with ARM & HAMMER® Baking Soda, then fill as usual with litter. To freshen between changes, sprinkle ARM & HAMMER® Baking Soda on top of the litter after a thorough cleaning. For even stronger litter box deodorization, try ARM & HAMMER® Cat Litter Deodorizer specially formulated to effectively destroy cat litter box odors on contact. Keeps any litter smelling fresher, longer.

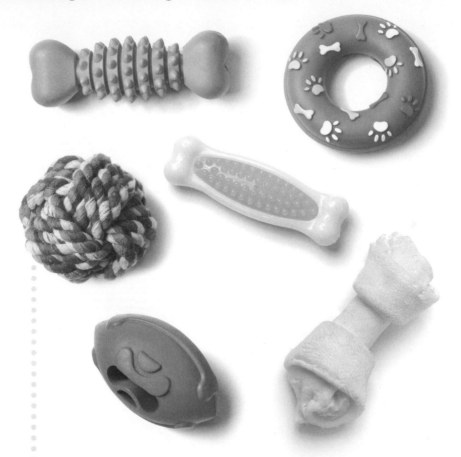

Dirty Pet Toys

Don't play catch with chemicals. Clean plastic and rubber toys safely by washing in a solution of ARM & HAMMER® Baking Soda (4 tablespoons dissolved in 1 quart of warm water). Give furry toys a dry shower by sprinkling ARM & HAMMER® Baking Soda on dry toys, and brushing off to thoroughly remove ARM & HAMMER® Baking Soda after 15 minutes.

Litter Box Odor

Litter box odor can spoil an otherwise clean, fresh home. Keep it under control with ARM & HAMMER® Cat Litter. Your family (and your cats) will thank you. Try ARM & HAMMER® Multi-Cat Extra Strength Clumping Litter for households with more than one cat. ARM & HAMMER® Essential® Natural Clumping Litter has virtually no dust and is made of natural corn fibers.

Freshen Pet Bedding

You love your pets, but you don't have to live with their odors. Eliminate odors from your pet's bedding by sprinkling liberally with ARM & HAMMER® Baking Soda, then wait 15 minutes (longer for stronger odors) and vacuum up thoroughly.*

*CAUTION: Before use, test hidden area of bedding for color-fastness. Mix ½ tablespoon in ½ cup water and pour small amount on bedding. Let dry, vacuum, and check bedding.

Chapter 5

Bathroom Cleaning & Freshening

ARM & HAMMER® Baking Soda is the safe, effective way to leave your whole bathroom sparkling clean and smelling fresh, without the need for harsh chemicals. You can even use ARM & HAMMER® Baking Soda on high-gloss surfaces like fiberglass and tiles without worrying about scratches!

Surface-Safe Cleaning
Glub in the tub? For safe, effective cleaning of bathroom tubs, tile, and sinks—even shiny fiberglass and glossy tiles— sprinkle ARM & HAMMER® Baking Soda lightly on a clean damp sponge and scrub as usual. Rinse thoroughly and wipe dry. Afterwards, take a nice relaxing bath.

Deodorizing Wastebasket
Defeating odors in the bathroom often feels like a waste of time. Keep bathroom wastebaskets fresh-smelling with just a sprinkle of ARM & HAMMER® Baking Soda. Apply regularly as you add to the container, or when you empty it, wash the container with a solution of 1 cup of ARM & HAMMER® Baking Soda per 1 gallon of water.

Septic Care
Regular use of ARM & HAMMER® Baking Soda in your drains can help keep your septic system flowing freely. We recommend adding 1 cup of ARM & HAMMER® Baking Soda per week to help maintain a favorable pH in your septic tank.

Shower Curtains
Clean and deodorize your vinyl shower curtain by sprinkling ARM & HAMMER® Baking Soda directly on a clean, damp sponge or brush. Scrub the shower curtain and rinse clean. Hang it up to dry.

Deodorizing Drains

What goes down sometimes comes back up. To deodorize your sink and tub drains, and keep lingering odors from resurfacing, pour ARM & HAMMER® Baking Soda down the drain (½ cup) while running warm tap water. ARM & HAMMER® Baking Soda will neutralize both acid and basic odors for a fresh drain. Here's a tidbit to remember: When replacing your box of ARM & HAMMER® Baking Soda Fridge-n-Freezer® Odor Absorber (every 30 days), pour the contents of the old box down the drain to get a little extra mileage.

Cleaning Bathroom Floors

Leave it up to ARM & HAMMER® Baking Soda to speed things up in the bathroom. ARM & HAMMER® Baking Soda helps remove the dirt and grime from bathroom tiles or no-wax floors quickly and easily. Mix ½ cup ARM & HAMMER® Baking Soda in a bucket of warm water, mop, and rinse clean for a sparkling floor.

Chapter 6

Laundry, Carpets, Floors & Household Use

No other product does more throughout your home than ARM & HAMMER® Baking Soda, so think outside of the box to help boost the cleaning and freshening power of your laundry detergent and remove crayon marks from walls. With so many solutions, there's almost nothing ARM & HAMMER® Baking Soda can't do!

Laundry Booster

Give your laundry a boost—then give yourself a hand! Add ½ cup of ARM & HAMMER® Baking Soda to your laundry to make liquid detergent work harder for you and your family. A better balance of pH in the wash gets clothes cleaner, fresher, brighter! Our large size resealable pouch size makes it an easy additive for every wash load.

Cleaning Furniture

Being sent to your room never looked so good. Clean and remove marks (even crayon!) from walls and painted furniture by applying ARM & HAMMER® Baking Soda to a damp sponge and rubbing lightly. Wipe off with a clean, dry cloth.

Carpet Odors

Sprinkle ARM & HAMMER® Baking Soda directly on carpets and wait 15 minutes before vacuuming thoroughly. You'll freshen your carpets while eliminating household odors.*

*CAUTION: Before use, test hidden area of carpet for color-fastness. Mix ½ tablespoon in ½ cup water and pour small amount on carpet. Let dry, vacuum, and check carpet.

Freshen Sheets

Get towels and linens clothesline fresh—right from the wash! Add ½ cup of ARM & HAMMER® Baking Soda to the rinse cycle and get ready for the great outdoors.

Freshen Closets

Just like the refrigerator, your closets can collect stale smells. So the ARM & HAMMER® Baking Soda Fridge-n-Freezer® Odor Absorber box does double duty here too! Place a box on the shelf to keep the closet smelling fresh. Remember to replace it every 30 days for optimal freshness!

Musty Towels

Fun in the sun can make towels smell musty. Get pool towels clothesline fresh—right from the wash! Add ½ cup ARM & HAMMER® Baking Soda to the rinse cycle.

Laundry Stains

Tough laundry stains need a tough laundry solution. Remove strong dirt and stains like blood, grass, and sauce with ARM & HAMMER® Plus OxiClean® Laundry Detergent. ARM & HAMMER® Plus OxiClean® Laundry Detergent combines OxiClean® stain removers with the cleaning and freshening power of ARM & HAMMER® Baking Soda.

Cleaning Floors

With all the pitter-patter of little feet in the kitchen, your floor is bound to get dirty. Remove dirt and grime (without unwanted scratch marks!) from no-wax and tile floors using ½ cup ARM & HAMMER® Baking Soda in a bucket of warm water; mop and rinse clean for a sparkling floor. For unsightly scuff marks, use ARM & HAMMER® Baking Soda on a clean, damp sponge, then rinse. Great for high-traffic areas and after dinner parties too!

Clean and Freshen Sports Gear

Be a good sport. Use an
ARM & HAMMER® Baking Soda
solution (4 tablespoons
ARM & HAMMER® Baking
Soda in 1 quart warm water)
to clean and deodorize
smelly sports equipment like
fishing and camping gear.
Sprinkle ARM & HAMMER®
Baking Soda into golf bags and
gym bags to deodorize and—
abbra caddabra—the odors are gone!
Clean golf irons (without scratching
them!) with an ARM & HAMMER® Baking
Soda paste (3 parts ARM & HAMMER®
Baking Soda to 1 part water) and a brush.
Rinse thoroughly and let dry.

Deodorize Gym Bags

Put an ARM & HAMMER® Baking Soda Fridge-n-Freezer® Odor Absorber box in your gym locker—and another in your gym bag! The removable front and back flaps let air flow through the box without messy spills!

Upholstery Spills

Pet accidents, kid accidents, even adult accidents— clean spills or accidents on upholstery by soaking up as much of the liquid as possible. Clean the stain according to the manufacturer's directions and allow to dry. Then to deodorize, when the area is completely dry, sprinkle with ARM & HAMMER® Baking Soda and let sit for 15 minutes before vacuuming it up. Check for color-fastness first before applying ARM & HAMMER® Baking Soda.*

*CAUTION: Before use, test hidden area of upholstery for color-fastness. Mix ½ tablespoon in ½ cup water and pour small amount on upholstery. Let dry, vacuum, and check upholstery.

Freshen Ashtrays

Cover up smells by sprinkling ARM & HAMMER® Baking Soda in the bottom of ashtrays. Replace the Baking Soda when you empty the ashtray. As an added bonus, the ARM & HAMMER® Baking Soda helps extinguish cigarettes and cigars!

Freshen Upholstery

Something neat for your seat! Keep comfy upholstered sofas and chairs smelling fresh with ARM & HAMMER® Baking Soda. Sprinkle Baking Soda on upholstery, wait 15 minutes, and vacuum up.*

*CAUTION: Before use, test hidden area of upholstery for color-fastness. Mix ½ tablespoon in ½ cup water and pour small amount on upholstery. Let dry, vacuum, and check upholstery.

Allergens

Stale air can be unpleasant and unhealthy. ARM & HAMMER® Air Filters in your home's heating & cooling system neutralize common household odors and capture airborne allergens, viruses, and more.

Deodorize Garbage Can

A couple of shakes is all it takes! Keep unpleasant smells to a minimum by sprinkling ARM & HAMMER® Baking Soda in the garbage between layers as they accumulate. Periodically wash out and deodorize garbage cans with a solution of 1 cup of ARM & HAMMER® Baking Soda per 1 gallon of water.

Recyclables

Keep those recyclables smelling fresh until collection day. Sprinkle ARM & HAMMER® Baking Soda on top as you add to the container.

Also, clean your recyclable container periodically by sprinkling ARM & HAMMER® Baking Soda on a damp sponge. Wipe clean and rinse.

Silver Tarnish Remover

Place a sheet of aluminum foil in the bottom of a baking pan. Sprinkle 1 to 2 teaspoons of ARM & HAMMER® Baking Soda and ½ teaspoon of salt on the foil. Add about 5 cups of boiling water to the pan to dissolve the ARM & HAMMER® Baking Soda and salt. Carefully (water will be very hot) place the tarnished silverware in the solution, making sure the silverware touches the aluminum foil. Let it stand for 2 to 3 minutes and carefully remove. Rinse the silverware well, and then use a soft cloth to buff dry. (We recommend polishing after tarnish removal to protect your silverware for future use.)

Flower Vases

To clean glass vases you've used for your beautiful flowers, fill three-quarters full with hot water, add a teaspoon of ARM & HAMMER® Baking Soda, and shake. Let sit, then rinse.

Fireplaces

Clean smoky buildup from your glass fireplace or wood-burning stove or oven. Crumple a piece of newspaper, wet it with water, and sprinkle some ARM & HAMMER® Baking Soda on it. Rub the dirty area of the glass and wipe it down with a damp, clean cloth. The residue will come off without scratching the glass.

Chapter 7

Kitchen & Cooking

ARM & HAMMER® Baking Soda goes way beyond freshening the fridge and freezer—it's the original kitchen multi-tasker. It can help you safely clean fruits and vegetables for your favorite meals, and then make washing pots and pans easier by lifting away baked-on food. It is the ultimate solution for cleaning stainless surfaces without scratching for a sparkling kitchen. And, ARM & HAMMER® Baking Soda is the secret for delicious baked goodies!

Funky Fridge

A funky fridge can spoil the flavor of your fresh food. Change the ARM & HAMMER® Baking Soda box every 30 days to stop flavor transfer and keep foods tasting fresher, longer. Don't wait until your food tells you, change it today.

Greasy Dishes

Greasy dishes overwhelm even the most effective detergents. To cut through the toughest grease, add 2 heaping tablespoons of ARM & HAMMER® Baking Soda to detergent and dishwater. Let pans soak for 15 minutes, then clean.

Dirty Microwave

Dirty microwaves retain the odor of everything we cook in them. For instant cleaning and deodorizing, sprinkle ARM & HAMMER® Baking Soda on a damp sponge and gently wipe the inside and outside of your microwave. To keep odors at bay, place a box of ARM & HAMMER® Baking Soda Fridge-N-Freezer® Odor Absorber in the microwave between uses—don't forget to replace it every 30 days for maximum freshness.

Dishwashers

Sprinkle ARM & HAMMER® Baking Soda in the bottom of the dishwasher to absorb food odors just lingering in the dishwasher. Double duty! Use ARM & HAMMER® Baking Soda to deodorize before you run the dishwasher.

Tomatoes

Cut the acidic level of tomato sauce or chili by adding a pinch of ARM & HAMMER® Baking Soda.

Coffee Maker

A cleaner coffee maker is a simple soak away. Just add ¼ cup ARM & HAMMER® Baking Soda to 1 quart of warm water to clean coffee makers, mugs, and more. For really tough stains, add dishwasher detergent and soak them in this solution overnight. Then simply sprinkle ARM & HAMMER® Baking Soda on a damp sponge and gently wipe away stains. Rinse thoroughly.

Canning Tips

Clean mineral deposits and neutralize any acids in old canning jars by shaking an ARM & HAMMER® Baking Soda solution inside. Rinse thoroughly, then sterilize as usual.

Clean & Deodorize Lunch Boxes

Keep today's egg salad from tasting like yesterday's tuna. Between uses, place a spill-proof box of ARM & HAMMER® Baking Soda Fridge-N-Freezer® Odor Absorber in everyone's lunch box.

Pots & Pans

Eliminate the heavy burden of scrubbing pots and pans! ARM & HAMMER® Baking Soda penetrates and helps lift off baked-on, dried-on foods. Shake on a generous amount of ARM & HAMMER® Baking Soda, add dish detergent and hot water; let sit for 15 minutes and wash as usual.

Fruit & Vegetable Scrub

An apple a day—cleaned the food-safe way!
ARM & HAMMER® Baking Soda is the food safe way to
clean dirt and residue off fresh fruit and vegetables. Just
sprinkle a little on a vegetable brush or a clean, damp
sponge, scrub, and rinse.

Surface Cleaning

Clean your food prep area with natural, food-safe
ARM & HAMMER® Baking Soda instead of harsh
cleaners. Sprinkle ARM & HAMMER® Baking Soda onto
a clean damp sponge or cloth and wipe clean, rinse
thoroughly, then dry. Great for counters, stainless steel
sinks, cutting boards, microwaves, plastic containers,
lunch boxes, back splashes, oven tops, range hoods,
and more!

Sponges

Here's something to soak in! Soak stale-smelling sponges
in a strong ARM & HAMMER® Baking Soda solution
(4 tablespoons of ARM & HAMMER® Baking Soda
dissolved in 1 quart of warm water) to get rid of the mess
and bring in the fresh.

Plastic Containers

Keep foods stored in plastic containers from
tasting like the last leftovers. Wash the containers
in between uses with ARM & HAMMER® Baking
Soda sprinkled on a clean, damp sponge. For
even tougher odors, just soak items in a solution of 4
tablespoons ARM & HAMMER® Baking Soda dissolved in
1 quart warm water.

Deodorizing Freezers

Fresh is best! To help keep foods tasting like they should, replace your ARM & HAMMER® Baking Soda Fridge-N-Freezer® Odor Absorber every 30 days. The unique flow-thru vents expose twice the amount of Baking Soda to absorb the odors that can make other foods (even ice cubes!) taste funky.

Fluffier Mashed Potatoes

With weather getting cooler, we turn to our favorite comfort foods. Throw a pinch of ARM & HAMMER® Baking Soda into potatoes while mashing to make them fluffier.

Baking

Make sure your baked goods "rise" to the occasion! ARM & HAMMER® Baking Soda is widely used as an agent to promote leavening. As ARM & HAMMER® Baking Soda is heated, it releases carbon dioxide, which causes dough or batter to rise, becoming light and porous. For more than 160 years, great bakers have trusted ARM & HAMMER® Baking Soda because it is made with the highest standards.

Silver Polish

What a bright idea! ARM & HAMMER® Baking Soda can shine all your silver in no time at all. Use a Baking Soda paste made with 3 parts ARM & HAMMER® Baking Soda to 1 part water. Rub onto the silver with a clean cloth or sponge. Rinse thoroughly and dry for shining sterling and silver-plate serving pieces. You'll be polished and ready to go for your next dinner party!

Tea Pots

Here's a quick pick-me-up! Remove tea stains and eliminate bitter off-tastes by washing mugs and tea pots in a solution of ¼ cup ARM & HAMMER® Baking Soda in 1 quart of warm water. For stubborn stains, try soaking overnight in the ARM & HAMMER® Baking Soda solution and detergent or scrubbing with ARM & HAMMER® Baking Soda on a clean, damp sponge.

Clean Mushrooms

Avoid soaking mushrooms when cleaning because they will retain water. Instead, wipe them clean with a damp cloth and just a sprinkle of ARM & HAMMER® Baking Soda.

Prepare Potatoes

Add a sprinkle of ARM & HAMMER® Baking Soda to each potato and then scrub using a brush. Dip in water while scrubbing and towel dry for a dirt-free potato that can be roasted and enjoyed skin-on.

Clean Produce Naturally

To remove dirt, wax, and residue from hard-skinned produce, shake ARM & HAMMER® Baking Soda onto wet produce. Rub and rinse. For soft-skinned or leafy produce, sprinkle Baking Soda in a bowl of water. Add produce, agitate, and rinse.

Chapter 8

The Backyard & Beyond

ARM & HAMMER® Baking Soda is ready for tough jobs—even in the garage and outside your home. Make it a part of your outdoor fun, from quick and easy pool care for a crystal clear pool, to a spotless grill and patio furniture for relaxing. ARM & HAMMER® Baking Soda even helps you clean and freshen inside and outside your car!

Camping Necessity

And you thought the tent was essential.
ARM & HAMMER® Baking Soda is a must-have for your next camping trip! One box does so much. It's a dishwasher, pot scrubber, hand cleanser, deodorant, toothpaste, and has tons of other uses.

Grimy Pool Toys

Grimy pool toys can ruin a perfectly beautiful day at the pool. Mix ¼ cup ARM & HAMMER® Baking Soda with 1 quart of warm water. Wipe down toys with the solution and rinse. Smaller items may be soaked first and then rinsed.

Easy Pool Care

Come on in, the water's fine! Improve your pool's clarity with ARM & HAMMER® Baking Soda. It's all about the pH. Dive right into our waterproof and resealable large size bags to keep pool water sparkling. (Follow usage directions printed right on the bag.)

Grungy Grills

Grungy grills aren't a welcome part of any backyard barbecue. Clean them up by sprinkling dry ARM & HAMMER® Baking Soda on a damp brush, scrub as needed, and rinse clean. For tough, greasy stains, scrub with a wire brush and a Baking Soda paste (3 parts Baking Soda to 1 part warm water), and rinse thoroughly.

Lawn Furniture

Get ready for your outdoor oasis! Before you pull out your outdoor patio and pool furniture for the season, give it a thorough cleaning with ARM & HAMMER® Baking Soda. And don't forget to keep outdoor furniture fresh in the off-season too—just sprinkle ARM & HAMMER® Baking Soda underneath cushions or inside the storage bag.

Cleaning Door and Window Screens

Before installing door and window screens you've been storing all winter, give them a quick scrub. Dip a damp wire brush into ARM & HAMMER® Baking Soda and scrub screens clean. Rinse with a sponge or hose.

Oil and Grease Stains

Use ARM & HAMMER® Baking Soda to clean up light-duty oil and grease spills on your garage floor or in your driveway. Sprinkle ARM & HAMMER® Baking Soda on the spot and scrub with a wet brush.

Cleaning Cars

Hit the road with ARM & HAMMER® Baking Soda! Use ARM & HAMMER® Baking Soda to safely clean your car lights, chrome, windows, tires, vinyl seats, and floor mats without worrying about unwanted scratch marks. Use an ARM & HAMMER® Baking Soda solution of ¼ cup Baking Soda in 1 quart of warm water. Apply with a sponge or soft cloth to remove road grime, tree sap, bugs, and tar. For stubborn stains, use ARM & HAMMER® Baking Soda sprinkled on a damp sponge or soft brush.

Cleaning Windshields

After a road trip, remove bugs from your car windshield by making a paste of ARM & HAMMER® Baking Soda and water, and applying with a damp, clean cloth.

Deodorizing Cars

Leave car odors in the dust! Odors settle into car upholstery and carpet, so each time you step in and sit down, they are released into the air all over again. Eliminate these odors by sprinkling ARM & HAMMER® Baking Soda directly on fabric car seats and carpets.

Wait 15 minutes (or longer for strong odors) and vacuum up the odors with the ARM & HAMMER® Baking Soda. Check for color-fastness first before applying ARM & HAMMER® Baking Soda.*

CAUTION: Before use, test hidden area of car seats and carpets for color-fastness. Mix ½ tablespoon in ½ cup water and pour small amount on car seats and carpets. Let dry, vacuum, and check car seats and carpet.

Deodorizing Camper Water Tanks

Freshen your RV water tank periodically by flushing with 1 cup ARM & HAMMER® Baking Soda dissolved in 1 gallon warm water. Drain and flush the tank before refilling (do not use ARM & HAMMER® Baking Soda in your drinking water). The ARM & HAMMER® Baking Soda will eliminate stale odors and help remove mineral build-up that makes water taste off.

Index

100 BEST

Holiday

APPETIZERS

Publications International, Ltd.

Favorite Brand Name Recipes at www.fbnr.com

Microwave Cooking: Microwave ovens vary in wattage. Use the cooking times as guidelines and check for doneness before adding more time.

Preparation/Cooking Times: Preparation times are based on the approximate amount of time required to assemble the recipe before cooking, baking, chilling or serving. These times include preparation steps such as measuring, chopping and mixing. The fact that some preparations and cooking can be done simultaneously is taken into account. Preparation of optional ingredients and serving suggestions is not included.

Contents

Delicious Dips & Spreads

Southern Pimiento Cheese

1 package (3 ounces) cream cheese, softened
⅓ cup HELLMANN'S® or BEST FOODS® Real Mayonnaise
2 cups shredded Cheddar cheese (about 8 ounces)
½ cup drained and chopped pimientos (about 4 ounces)
½ cup finely chopped green onions
¼ cup finely chopped pimiento-stuffed green olives
1 teaspoon LAWRY'S® Garlic Powder with Parsley
1 teaspoon paprika

1. In medium bowl, with wire whisk, beat cream cheese and Hellmann's or Best Foods Real Mayonnaise until smooth. Stir in remaining ingredients until blended. Chill until ready to serve.

2. Serve at room temperature and, if desired, with crackers or party-size bread. *Makes 2¼ cups spread*

Prep Time: 15 minutes
Chill Time: 30 minutes

Clockwise from top left: Holiday Cheese Tree (page 24), Spicy Thai Satay Dip (page 30), Southern Pimiento Cheese and Roasted Garlic Hummus (page 16)

4

Santa Fe Pineapple Salsa

2 cups finely chopped fresh DOLE® Tropical Gold® Pineapple
1 can (8 ounces) red, pinto or kidney beans, rinsed and drained
1 can (8¼ ounces) whole kernel corn, drained
1 cup chopped green or red bell pepper
½ cup finely chopped DOLE® Red Onion
2 tablespoons chopped fresh cilantro
1 to 2 teaspoons seeded and chopped fresh jalapeño pepper
½ teaspoon grated lime peel
2 tablespoons lime juice

• Combine pineapple, beans, corn, bell pepper, onion, cilantro, jalapeño, lime peel and juice in medium serving bowl. Cover and chill at least 30 minutes to allow flavors to blend. Serve with grilled salmon and asparagus. Garnish with grilled pineapple wedges, if desired.

• Salsa can also be served as a dip with tortilla chips or spooned over quesadillas or tacos. *Makes 10 servings*

Prep Time: 20 minutes
Chill Time: 30 minutes

Feta Avocado Spread

4 ripe avocados, peeled and cut into chunks
1 (4-ounce) package feta cheese, crumbled
1 tablespoon olive oil
  Juice of 1 lemon
2 teaspoons TABASCO® brand Green Jalapeño Pepper Sauce
  Salt to taste
1 baguette French bread *or* 2 heads Belgian endive (optional)

Combine avocados, feta cheese, oil, lemon juice, TABASCO® Green Sauce and salt in medium bowl. Mix with fork until well blended and still slightly lumpy. Spoon into serving bowl and refrigerate until ready to serve.

Serve with sliced baguette rounds, if desired. For more elegant presentation, spoon small amount of spread on larger ends of endive leaves and arrange on platter. *Makes 3½ cups*

Santa Fe Pineapple Salsa

Pepperoni Pizza Dip

1 jar or can (14 ounces) pizza sauce
¾ cup chopped turkey pepperoni
4 green onions, chopped
1 can (2¼ ounces) sliced black olives, drained
½ teaspoon dried oregano
1 cup (4 ounces) shredded mozzarella cheese
1 package (3 ounces) cream cheese, softened
   Breadstick Dippers (recipe follows)

Slow Cooker Directions
1. Combine pizza sauce, pepperoni, green onions, olives and oregano in 2-quart slow cooker. Cover; cook on LOW 2 hours or on HIGH 1 to 1½ hours or until mixture is hot.

2. Stir in mozzarella and cream cheese until melted and well blended. Serve with Breadstick Dippers. *Makes 8 servings*

Breadstick Dippers

1 package (8 ounces) refrigerated breadstick dough
2 teaspoons melted butter
2 teaspoons minced parsley

Bake breadsticks according to package directions. Brush with melted butter and sprinkle with parsley. Serve with warm dip. *Makes 8 breadsticks*

Pear Walnut Cheese Spread

1 can (15 ounces) Bartlett pears, finely diced
½ cup toasted walnuts, chopped
2 tablespoons chopped fresh chives
1 cup (4 ounces) crumbled blue cheese

Combine pears, walnuts and chives in medium bowl. Stir in blue cheese. Serve as a dip with crackers or toasted pita bread triangles.
Makes 2 cups spread

*Favorite recipe from **Pacific Northwest Canned Pear Service***

Pepperoni Pizza Dip

Olive Tapenade

1 can (16 ounces) medium pitted black olives
½ cup pimiento-stuffed green olives
1 tablespoon roasted garlic*
½ teaspoon dry mustard
½ cup (2 ounces) crumbled feta cheese
1 tablespoon olive oil
    Toasted bread slices

To roast garlic, preheat oven to 400°F. Remove outer layers of papery skin and cut ¼ inch off top of garlic head. Place cut side up on a piece of heavy-duty foil. Drizzle with 2 teaspoons olive oil; wrap tightly in foil. Bake 25 to 30 minutes or until cloves feel soft when pressed. Cool slightly before squeezing out garlic pulp.

1. Process olives, roasted garlic and mustard in food processor or blender until finely chopped.

2. Combine olive mixture, feta cheese and oil in medium bowl; stir until well blended. Serve with toasted bread.   *Makes 1¾ cups dip*

Tip: For the best flavor, prepare this tapenade several hours or one day ahead to allow the flavors to blend.

Black Bean & Roasted Red Pepper Dip

1 package (1 ounce) LAWRY'S® Taco Spices & Seasonings
1 can (15 ounces) black beans, rinsed and drained
1 jar (7 ounces) roasted red peppers, drained
12 ounces cream cheese, softened
1 tablespoon chopped fresh cilantro
1 to 2 teaspoons lime juice

Garnishes
    Chopped tomato or bell pepper and fresh cilantro

In food processor combine all ingredients until smooth. Garnish, if desired, with chopped tomato or bell pepper and chopped fresh cilantro, and serve with tortilla chips or assorted raw vegetables.   *Makes 3 cups dip*

Prep Time: 10 minutes

Olive Tapenade

Pesto Cheese Wreath

Parsley-Basil Pesto* (recipe follows)
3 packages (8 ounces each) cream cheese, softened
½ cup mayonnaise
¼ cup whipping cream or half-and-half
1 teaspoon sugar
1 teaspoon onion salt
⅓ cup chopped roasted red peppers** or pimiento, drained
   Pimiento strips and Italian flat leaf parsley (optional)
   Cut-up vegetables or assorted crackers

*One-half cup purchased pesto can be substituted for Parsley-Basil Pesto.
**Look for roasted red peppers packed in jars or cans in the Italian food section
of the supermarket.

1. Prepare Parsley-Basil Pesto; set aside. Beat cream cheese and mayonnaise
in medium bowl until smooth; beat in cream, sugar and onion salt.

2. Line 5-cup ring mold with plastic wrap. Spoon half of cheese mixture
into prepared mold; spread evenly. Spread Parsley-Basil Pesto evenly over
cheese mixture; top with roasted peppers. Spoon remaining cheese mixture
over peppers; spread evenly. Cover; refrigerate until cheese mixture is firm,
8 hours or overnight.

3. Uncover mold; invert onto serving plate. Carefully remove plastic wrap.
Smooth top and sides of wreath with spatula. Garnish with pimiento strips
and parsley. Serve with vegetables.   *Makes 16 to 24 servings*

Parsley-Basil Pesto: Combine 2 cups fresh parsley, ¼ cup pine nuts or
slivered almonds, 2 tablespoons grated Parmesan cheese, 2 cloves garlic,
1 teaspoon dried basil and ¼ teaspoon salt in food processor or blender.
Process until finely chopped. With machine running, add 2 tablespoons
olive oil gradually, processing until mixture is smooth.

Pesto Cheese Wreath

Onion & White Bean Spread

1 can (about 15 ounces) cannellini or Great Northern beans,
   rinsed and drained
¼ cup chopped green onions
¼ cup grated Parmesan cheese
¼ cup olive oil
1 tablespoon fresh rosemary leaves, finely chopped
2 cloves garlic, minced
   Additional olive oil
   French bread slices

1. Combine beans, green onions, Parmesan, oil, rosemary and garlic in food processor; process 30 to 40 seconds or until mixture is almost smooth.

2. Spoon bean mixture into serving bowl. Drizzle additional olive oil over spread just before serving. Serve with bread.   *Makes 1¼ cups spread*

Tip: For a more rustic spread, place all ingredients in a medium bowl and mash with a potato masher.

Mexican Fiesta Dip

1 can (16 ounces) refried beans
3 avocados, chopped
2 teaspoons lemon juice
   Salt and pepper to taste
1 pint sour cream
1¾ cups (7 ounces) SARGENTO® Bistro® Blends Shredded Chipotle
   Cheddar Cheese, divided
1 bunch green onions, chopped
2 tomatoes, seeded and chopped
1 can (2¼ ounces) sliced black olives, drained
   Tortilla chips

1. Spread refried beans on large platter. Combine avocados, lemon juice, salt and pepper and spoon mixture on top of beans. Combine sour cream and 1 cup cheese. Spread on top of avocado mixture.

2. Combine green onions, tomatoes and olives. Spread mixture in ring around outside edge of platter. Garnish top with remaining cheese and serve with tortilla chips.   *Makes 6 servings*

Onion & White Bean Spread

Blue Cheese Dip for Pears

1 package (8 ounces) cream cheese, softened
⅓ cup KARO® Light or Dark Corn Syrup
2 teaspoons lemon juice
⅛ teaspoon ground ginger
½ cup (2 ounces) crumbled blue cheese
3 pears, thinly sliced

1. In small bowl with mixer at medium speed, beat cream cheese, corn syrup, lemon juice and ginger until smooth. Stir in blue cheese until mixed.

2. Cover; chill 1 to 2 hours.

3. Garnish with additional blue cheese crumbles. Serve with sliced fresh pears.   *Makes about 1½ cups dip*

Roasted Garlic Hummus

2 tablespoons Roasted Garlic (recipe follows)
1 can (15 ounces) chickpeas, rinsed and drained
¼ cup fresh parsley sprigs
2 tablespoons water
2 tablespoons lemon juice
½ teaspoon curry powder
⅛ teaspoon dark sesame oil
   Dash hot pepper sauce
   Pita bread and fresh vegetables

1. Prepare Roasted Garlic.

2. Place chickpeas, parsley, 2 tablespoons Roasted Garlic, water, lemon juice, curry powder, sesame oil and hot pepper sauce in food processor or blender. Cover; process until smooth.

3. Serve with pita bread and fresh vegetables.   *Makes 6 servings*

Roasted Garlic: Cut off top third of 1 large garlic head (not the root end) to expose cloves; discard top. Place head of garlic, trimmed end up, on 10-inch square of foil. Rub garlic generously with olive oil and sprinkle with salt. Gather foil ends together and close tightly. Roast in preheated 350°F oven 45 minutes or until cloves are golden and soft. When cool enough to handle, squeeze roasted garlic cloves from skins; discard skins.

Blue Cheese Dip for Pears

Robust Cheddar, Feta and Walnut Cheese Log

8 ounces (2 cups) grated California Cheddar cheese
8 ounces (1 cup) cream cheese
4 ounces (¾ cup) crumbled California feta cheese
2 cloves garlic, minced
¼ teaspoon salt
¼ teaspoon hot pepper sauce
1 cup chopped California walnuts, toasted, if desired, divided
2 tablespoons capers, drained
2 tablespoons chopped, roasted and peeled red bell pepper *or*
        2 tablespoons chopped pimientos
2 tablespoons gin or vodka (optional)
    Pinch cayenne pepper

Combine Cheddar cheese, cream cheese, feta cheese, garlic, salt and pepper sauce; mix until blended and smooth. Add ½ cup walnuts, capers, bell pepper and gin, if desired. Continue to mix until ingredients are incorporated and evenly blended. Mixture will be easier to shape if refrigerated 2 to 3 hours before forming.

Add cayenne pepper to remaining ½ cup walnuts and toss to coat. Spread nuts on sheet of waxed paper.

With damp hands, divide cheese mixture in half. Pat and press each half into ball about 3 inches across or into log about 5 inches long and 2 inches wide. (Shape does not need to be perfect.)

Roll each log or ball in walnuts, patting coating in firmly. Wrap in plastic wrap and chill until ready to serve.   *Makes 12 servings*

Feta and Fontina Walnut Cheese Ball: Omit the Cheddar and cream cheese and substitute 8 ounces (2 cups) grated California fontina cheese and 4 ounces (1 cup) grated California mozzarella cheese. Combine with the feta cheese and other ingredients as directed above. If desired, roll the balls or logs in a mixture of ¼ cup chopped parsley and ¼ cup dry bread crumbs or rye cracker crumbs.

*Favorite recipe from **Walnut Marketing Board***

Robust Cheddar, Feta and Walnut Cheese Log

Cucumber-Dill Dip

Salt
1 cucumber, peeled, seeded and finely chopped
6 green onions, white parts only, chopped
1 cup plain yogurt
1 package (3 ounces) cream cheese
2 tablespoons fresh dill *or* 1 tablespoon dried dill weed
Fresh dill sprigs (optional)

1. Lightly salt cucumber in small bowl; toss. Refrigerate 1 hour. Drain and dry on paper towels. Return cucumber to bowl; stir in green onions.

2. Place yogurt, cream cheese and dill in food processor or blender; process until smooth. Stir into cucumber mixture. Transfer to serving bowl. Cover; refrigerate 1 hour. Garnish with fresh dill.   *Makes about 2 cups dip*

Pumpkin Chile Cheese Dip

1 tablespoon butter
¼ cup finely chopped green bell pepper
2 tablespoons finely chopped onion
1 cup solid-pack pumpkin
1 can (10¾ ounces) condensed nacho cheese soup,* undiluted
½ cup half-and-half
1 to 2 teaspoons minced canned chipotle chile in adobo sauce
¼ teaspoon salt

*If nacho cheese soup is unavailable, substitute Cheddar cheese soup and add additional ½ teaspoon chipotle chile.

1. Melt butter in medium saucepan over medium heat. Add bell pepper and onion; cook and stir 3 minutes or until tender.

2. Stir in pumpkin, soup, half-and-half, 1 teaspoon chipotle chile and salt; cook over low heat 10 minutes, stirring frequently. Taste and add additional chile, if desired. Serve warm with tortilla chips and vegetables for dipping.
Makes about 2 cups dip

Note: Two teaspoons of chipotle chile will make the dip very hot. Start with 1 teaspoon, and taste before adding additional chile.

Cucumber-Dill Dip

Cheese Pinecones

2 cups (8 ounces) shredded Swiss cheese
½ cup (1 stick) butter, softened
3 tablespoons milk
2 tablespoons dry sherry or milk
⅛ teaspoon ground red pepper
1 cup finely chopped blanched almonds
¾ cup slivered blanched almonds
¾ cup sliced almonds
½ cup whole almonds
   Assorted crackers

1. Beat cheese, butter, milk, sherry and red pepper in medium bowl with electric mixer at low speed until smooth; stir in chopped almonds.

2. Divide mixture into 3 equal portions; shape each into tapered oval to resemble pinecone. Insert slivered, sliced or whole almonds into each cone. Cover; refrigerate 2 to 3 hours or until firm.

3. Arrange Cheese Pinecones on wooden board or serving plate. Serve with assorted crackers. *Makes 12 to 16 servings*

Olive & Feta Dip

1 cup HELLMANN'S® or BEST FOODS® Real Mayonnaise
4 ounces cream cheese, softened
3 ounces feta cheese, crumbled
⅓ cup chopped kalamata olives
3 green onions, chopped
1 clove garlic, pressed or finely chopped
¼ teaspoon dried oregano leaves, crushed

1. Preheat oven to 350°F.

2. In medium bowl combine all ingredients. Spoon into 1½-quart casserole.

3. Bake 30 minutes or until heated through. Serve with pita wedges or your favorite dippers. *Makes 2 cups dip*

Prep Time: 10 minutes
Cook Time: 30 minutes

Cheese Pinecones

Hot Crab-Cheddar Spread

1 (8-ounce) container crabmeat, drained and shredded
8 ounces CABOT® Mild or Sharp Cheddar, grated (about 2 cups)
½ cup mayonnaise
¼ teaspoon Worcestershire sauce

1. Preheat oven to 350°F.

2. In medium bowl, mix together all ingredients thoroughly. Transfer to small (1-quart) baking dish. Bake for 25 to 35 minutes or until lightly browned on top and bubbling at edges. Serve with crackers or bread toasts.
Makes 8 to 10 servings

Holiday Cheese Tree

1 package (8 ounces) cream cheese, softened
2 cups (8 ounces) shredded Cheddar cheese
3 tablespoons finely chopped red bell pepper
3 tablespoons finely chopped onion
1 tablespoon lemon juice
2 teaspoons Worcestershire sauce
¾ cup chopped fresh parsley
   Yellow bell pepper
   Cherry tomatoes, halved
   Pita Cutouts (recipe follows, optional)

1. Combine cream cheese, Cheddar cheese, red bell pepper, onion, lemon juice and Worcestershire sauce in medium bowl; stir until well blended. Shape into 6-inch-tall cone shape on serving plate. Press parsley evenly onto cheese tree.

2. Cut yellow bell pepper into desired shapes with cookie cutter or sharp knife. Press bell pepper shapes and tomatoes onto tree. Serve with Pita Cutouts, if desired.   *Makes about 5 cups spread (14 to 16 servings)*

Pita Cutouts: Split 6 pita bread rounds in half horizontally. Cut pitas into tree, star and bell shapes using 3-inch cutters or sharp knife. Place in single layer on ungreased baking sheet. Lightly brush with olive oil; sprinkle evenly with ¼ cup grated Parmesan cheese. Bake in preheated 350°F oven 15 to 20 minutes or until crisp. Remove to wire racks to cool completely.

Hot Crab-Cheddar Spread

Jalapeño Black Bean Dip

1 can (16 ounces) black beans, drained and mashed
1 cup shredded Monterey Jack or Cheddar cheese (about 4 ounces)
⅓ cup HELLMANN'S® or BEST FOODS® Real Mayonnaise
1 jalapeño pepper, finely chopped
½ teaspoon ground cumin
¼ teaspoon LAWRY'S® Garlic Powder with Parsley

1. Preheat oven to 375°F. In medium bowl, combine beans, ½ cup cheese, Hellmann's or Best Foods Real Mayonnaise, jalapeño, cumin and Garlic Powder with Parsley.

2. Spoon into 1-quart casserole, then top with remaining ½ cup cheese. Bake uncovered 20 minutes or until heated through. Serve with your favorite dippers.   *Makes 1½ cups dip*

Savory Seafood Spread

2 packages (8 ounces each) light cream cheese, softened
1 package (8 ounces) imitation crab meat, flaked
2 tablespoons minced green onion
1 tablespoon prepared horseradish
1 tablespoon *Frank's® RedHot®* Original Cayenne Pepper Sauce
1 teaspoon *French's®* Worcestershire Sauce
½ cup sliced almonds
  Paprika
  Crackers
  Vegetable dippers

1. Preheat oven to 375°F. Beat or process cream cheese in electric mixer or food processor until smooth and creamy. Add crab, onion, horseradish, ***Frank's RedHot*** Sauce and Worcestershire; beat or process until well blended.

2. Spread cream cheese mixture onto 9-inch pie plate. Top with almonds and sprinkle with paprika. Bake 20 minutes or until mixture is heated through and almonds are golden.

3. Serve with crackers or vegetable dippers.   *Makes 3 cups spread*

Jalapeño Black Bean Dip

Easy Cheese Fondue

1 pound low-sodium Swiss cheese (Gruyère, Emmentaler or
    combination of both), shredded or cubed
2 tablespoons cornstarch
1 clove garlic, minced
1 cup HOLLAND HOUSE® White or White with Lemon
    Cooking Wine
1 tablespoon kirsch or cherry brandy (optional)
    Pinch nutmeg
    Ground black pepper

1. In medium bowl, coat cheese with cornstarch; set aside. Rub inside of
ceramic fondue pot or heavy saucepan with garlic; discard garlic. Add wine
to fondue pot; bring to gentle simmer over medium heat. Gradually stir in
cheese to ensure smooth fondue. Once smooth, stir in brandy, if desired.
Garnish with nutmeg and pepper.

2. Serve with bite-sized chunks of French bread, broccoli, cauliflower,
tart apples or pears. Spear with fondue forks or wooden skewers.

Makes 1¼ cups fondue

Smoked Salmon Dip

4 ounces smoked salmon
1 container (8 ounces) whipped cream cheese
½ cup finely chopped tomatoes
¼ cup minced green onions, green parts only
2 teaspoons capers
    Unsalted pretzel crackers

1. Finely chop salmon or process in food processor until minced.

2. Place salmon in medium serving bowl. Stir in cream cheese, tomatoes,
green onions and capers; mix well. Serve with pretzel crackers.

Makes 1¾ cups dip

Tips: Don't use top-quality smoked salmon in this recipe; less expensive
salmon works well. The dip can be prepared one day in advance, covered
with plastic wrap and refrigerated.

Easy Cheese Fondue

Spicy Thai Satay Dip

⅓ cup peanut butter
⅓ cup *French's*® Honey Dijon Mustard
⅓ cup fat-free chicken broth
1 tablespoon chopped peeled fresh ginger
1 tablespoon honey
1 tablespoon *Frank's*® *RedHot*® Cayenne Pepper Sauce
1 tablespoon teriyaki sauce
1 tablespoon grated orange peel
2 cloves garlic, minced

1. Combine all ingredients in large bowl. Cover and refrigerate.

2. Serve with vegetables, chips or grilled meats.

Makes 4 (¼-cup) servings

Prep Time: 10 minutes

Caponata Spread

1½ tablespoons BERTOLLI® Olive Oil
1 medium eggplant, diced (about 4 cups)
1 medium onion, chopped
1½ cups water, divided
1 envelope LIPTON® RECIPE SECRETS® Savory Herb with Garlic
  Soup Mix
2 tablespoons chopped fresh parsley (optional)
  Salt and ground black pepper to taste
  Pita chips or thinly sliced Italian or French bread

1. In 10-inch nonstick skillet, heat oil over medium heat and cook eggplant with onion 3 minutes. Add ½ cup water. Reduce heat to low and simmer covered, 3 minutes.

2. Stir in soup mix blended with remaining 1 cup water. Bring to a boil over high heat. Reduce heat to low and simmer uncovered, stirring occasionally, 20 minutes.

3. Stir in parsley, salt and pepper. Serve with pita chips.

Makes about 4 cups spread

Cheddar Cheese Fruit Ball

¾ cup **SUN-MAID® Fruit Bits**
¼ cup **apple juice or white grape juice**
2 **(8-ounce) packages cream cheese, softened**
2 **tablespoons milk**
2 **cups finely shredded sharp Cheddar cheese**
¼ cup **thinly sliced green onions**
¾ cup **chopped walnuts**
    Crackers

COMBINE fruit bits and apple juice in a small saucepan. Bring to a simmer. Stir well and refrigerate 15 minutes.

BEAT cream cheese and milk with electric mixer or in food processor until fluffy.

ADD Cheddar cheese and green onions; beat or process until combined.

DRAIN fruit; add to cream cheese mixture, beating at low speed or with on/off pulses just until fruit is combined. Transfer mixture to a sheet of plastic wrap. Bring up edges of the plastic wrap; form the mixture into a 6-inch ball.

CHILL until firm, at least 2 hours or up to 24 hours. Just before serving, unwrap cheese and roll in walnuts. Serve with crackers.

Makes one 6-inch ball (about 12 servings)

Prep Time: 15 minutes
Chill Time: 2 hours

Guacamole

2 **avocados, mashed**
¼ cup **red salsa (mild or hot, according to taste)**
3 **tablespoons NEWMAN'S OWN® Salad Dressing**
2 **tablespoons lime or lemon juice**
1 **clove garlic, finely minced**
    Salt and black pepper

Combine all ingredients and mix well. Chill for 1 to 2 hours tightly covered. Serve with tortilla chips.

Makes about 2 cups

Spinach, Crab and Artichoke Dip

**1 package (10 ounces) frozen chopped spinach, thawed and squeezed
    nearly dry**
1 package (8 ounces) cream cheese
**1 jar (6 to 7 ounces) marinated artichoke hearts, drained and finely
    chopped**
1 can (6½ ounces) crabmeat, drained and shredded
¼ teaspoon hot pepper sauce

Slow Cooker Directions
Combine spinach, cream cheese, artichoke hearts, crabmeat and hot pepper
sauce in 1½-quart slow cooker. Cover and cook on HIGH 1½ to 2 hours
or until heated through, stirring after 1 hour. (Dip will stay warm in slow
cooker for 2 hours.)   *Makes 2½ cups dip*

Serving Suggestion: Serve with Melba toast or whole wheat crackers.

Zesty Pesto Cheese Spread

2 packages (8 ounces each) cream cheese, softened
1 cup shredded mozzarella cheese
1 cup chopped fresh basil or parsley
½ cup grated Parmesan cheese
½ cup toasted pine nuts*
⅓ cup *French's*® Honey Dijon Mustard
1 clove garlic

**To toast pine nuts, place nuts on baking sheet. Bake at 350°F 8 to 10 minutes or
until lightly golden or microwave in microwavable dish on HIGH (100%) 1 minute.*

1. Combine cream cheese, mozzarella, basil, Parmesan, pine nuts, mustard
and garlic in food processor. Cover and process until smooth and well
blended.

2. Spoon pesto spread into serving bowl or crock. Spread on crackers or
serve with vegetable crudites.   *Makes 3¼ cups spread*

Serving Variations: Pesto spread may also be piped into cherry tomatoes
using pastry bag fitted with decorative tip. Or, use as filling in rolled flour
tortillas.

Spinach, Crab and Artichoke Dip

Slow Cooker Cheese Dip

1 pound ground beef
1 pound bulk Italian sausage
1 package (16 ounces) pasteurized process cheese, cubed
1 can (11 ounces) sliced jalapeño peppers, drained
1 medium onion, diced
2 cups (8 ounces) Cheddar cheese, cubed
1 package (8 ounces) cream cheese, cubed
1 container (8 ounces) cottage cheese
1 container (8 ounces) sour cream
1 can (8 ounces) diced tomatoes, drained
3 cloves garlic, minced
Salt and black pepper

Slow Cooker Directions

1. Brown ground beef and sausage 6 to 8 minutes in medium skillet over medium-high heat, stirring to break up meat. Drain fat. Transfer meat to slow cooker.

2. Add process cheese, jalapeño peppers, onion, Cheddar cheese, cream cheese, cottage cheese, sour cream, tomatoes and garlic to slow cooker. Season with salt and black pepper.

3. Cover; cook on HIGH 1½ to 2 hours or until cheeses are melted. Serve with tortilla chips or crackers. *Makes 16 to 18 servings*

Sweet Pumpkin Dip

2 packages (8 ounces each) cream cheese, softened
1 can (15 ounces) LIBBY's® 100% Pure Pumpkin
2 cups sifted powdered sugar
1 teaspoon ground cinnamon
1 teaspoon ground ginger
Fresh sliced fruit, bite-size cinnamon graham crackers, gingersnap cookies, toasted mini bagels, toast slices, muffins or English muffins.

Beat cream cheese and pumpkin in large mixer bowl until smooth. Add sugar, cinnamon and ginger; mix thoroughly. Cover; refrigerate for 1 hour. Serve as a dip or spread. *Makes about 5½ cups*

Slow Cooker Cheese Dip

Party Favorites

Raspberry-Balsamic Glazed Meatballs

  1 bag (34 ounces) frozen fully cooked meatballs
  1 cup raspberry preserves
  3 tablespoons sugar
  3 tablespoons balsamic vinegar
1½ tablespoons Worcestershire sauce
  ¼ teaspoon red pepper flakes
  1 tablespoon grated fresh ginger (optional)

Slow Cooker Directions

1. Spray slow cooker with nonstick cooking spray. Add frozen meatballs; set aside.

2. Combine preserves, sugar, vinegar, Worcestershire sauce and red pepper flakes in small microwavable bowl. Microwave on HIGH 45 seconds. Stir; microwave 15 seconds or until melted (mixture will be chunky). Reserve ½ cup mixture. Pour remaining mixture over meatballs and toss gently to coat. Cover; cook on LOW 5 hours or on HIGH 2½ hours.

3. Turn slow cooker to HIGH. Stir in ginger, if desired, and reserved ½ cup preserve mixture. Cook, uncovered, 15 to 20 minutes or until thickened slightly, stirring occasionally.   *Makes about 12 servings*

Clockwise from top left: Cheesy Christmas Trees (page 62), Stuffed Mushroom Caps (page 61), Rasberry-Balsamic Glazed Meatballs and Appetizer Chicken Wings (page 38)

Easy Sausage Empanadas

1 (15-ounce) package refrigerated pie crusts (2 crusts)
¼ pound bulk pork sausage
2 tablespoons finely chopped onion
⅛ teaspoon garlic powder
⅛ teaspoon ground cumin
⅛ teaspoon dried oregano
1 tablespoon chopped pimiento-stuffed green olives
1 tablespoon chopped raisins
1 egg, separated

Let pie crusts stand at room temperature 20 minutes or according to package directions. Crumble sausage into medium skillet. Add onion, garlic powder, cumin and oregano; cook over medium-high heat until sausage is no longer pink. Drain drippings. Stir in olives and raisins. Lightly beat egg yolk; stir into sausage mixture, mixing well. Carefully unfold crusts. Cut into desired shapes using 3-inch cookie cutters. Place about 2 teaspoons sausage filling on half the cutouts. Top with remaining cutouts. (Or, use round cutter, top with sausage filling and fold dough over to create half-moon shape.) Moisten fingers with water and pinch dough to seal edges. Lightly beat egg white; gently brush over tops of empanadas. Bake in 425°F oven 15 to 18 minutes or until golden brown.   *Makes 12 appetizer servings*

*Favorite recipe from **National Pork Board***

Appetizer Chicken Wings

2½ to 3 pounds (12 to 14) chicken wings
1 cup (8 ounces) fat-free French dressing
½ cup KARO® Light or Dark Corn Syrup
1 package (1.4 ounces) French onion soup, dip and recipe mix
1 tablespoon Worcestershire sauce

Cut tips from wings and discard. Cut wings apart at joints and arrange in 13×9×2-inch baking pan lined with foil.

In medium bowl mix dressing, corn syrup, recipe mix and Worcestershire sauce; pour over wings.

Bake in 350°F oven 1 hour, stirring once, or until wings are tender.
Makes 24 servings

Easy Sausage Empanadas

Micro Mini Stuffed Potatoes

1 pound small new potatoes, scrubbed
¼ cup sour cream
2 tablespoons butter, softened
½ teaspoon minced garlic
¼ cup milk
½ cup (2 ounces) shredded sharp Cheddar cheese
½ teaspoon salt
¼ teaspoon black pepper
¼ cup finely chopped green onions (optional)

1. Pierce potatoes with fork in several places. Microwave potatoes on HIGH 5 to 6 minutes or until tender. Let stand 5 minutes; cut in half lengthwise. Scoop out pulp from potatoes and place in medium bowl.

2. Beat potatoes with electric mixer at low speed 30 seconds. Add sour cream, butter and garlic; beat until well blended. Gradually add milk, beating until smooth. Add cheese, salt and pepper; beat until blended.

3. Fill each potato shell with equal amounts of potato mixture. Microwave on HIGH 1 to 2 minutes or just until cheese melts. Garnish with green onions. *Makes 4 servings*

Cocktail Wraps

16 thin strips Cheddar cheese*
16 HILLSHIRE FARM® Lit'l Smokies, scored lengthwise
1 can (8 ounces) refrigerated crescent roll dough
1 egg, beaten *or* 1 tablespoon milk
Mustard

*Or substitute Swiss, taco-flavored or other variety of cheese.

Preheat oven to 400°F.

Place 1 strip cheese inside score of each Lit'l Smokie. Separate dough into 8 triangles; cut each lengthwise into halves to make 16 triangles. Place 1 link on wide end of 1 dough triangle; roll up. Repeat with remaining links and dough triangles. Place links on baking sheet. Brush dough with egg. Bake 10 to 15 minutes.

Serve hot with mustard. *Makes 16 hors d'oeuvres*

Micro Mini Stuffed Potatoes

Asparagus & Prosciutto Antipasto

12 asparagus spears (about 8 ounces)
2 ounces cream cheese, softened
¼ cup (1 ounce) crumbled blue cheese or goat cheese
¼ teaspoon black pepper
1 package (3 to 4 ounces) thinly sliced prosciutto

1. Trim and discard tough ends of asparagus spears. Simmer asparagus in salted water in large skillet 4 to 5 minutes or until crisp-tender. Drain; immediately immerse in cold water to stop cooking. Drain; pat dry with paper towels.

2. Meanwhile, combine cream cheese, blue cheese and pepper in small bowl; mix well. Cut prosciutto slices in half crosswise to make 12 pieces. Spread cream cheese mixture evenly over one side of each prosciutto slice.

3. Wrap each asparagus spear with one prosciutto slice. Serve at room temperature or slightly chilled. *Makes 12 appetizers*

Zesty Bruschetta

1 baguette French bread, cut into 1-inch slices
1 cup diced plum tomatoes, drained of excess juice
1 (4-ounce) package feta cheese, crumbled
2 to 3 green onions, chopped
¼ cup chopped black olives
2 tablespoons finely chopped fresh basil
1 teaspoon olive oil
½ teaspoon Original TABASCO® brand Pepper Sauce
Salt to taste
Fresh basil sprigs (optional)

Preheat broiler. Place bread slices on broiling pan and broil each side until lightly toasted. Set aside.

Gently combine remaining ingredients except basil sprigs in medium bowl until well blended. Top each bread slice generously with tomato mixture. Serve bruschetta on platter; garnish with basil sprigs, if desired.
Makes 20 to 24 pieces

Asparagus & Prosciutto Antipasto

One-Bite Burgers

1 package (11 ounces) refrigerated breadstick dough (12 breadsticks)
1 pound ground beef
2 teaspoons hamburger seasoning mix
    Cheddar or American cheese slices, quartered (optional)
36 dill pickle slices
    Ketchup or mustard

1. Preheat oven to 375°F. Separate dough into 12 breadsticks; cut each breadstick into 3 equal pieces. Working with one piece at a time, tuck ends under to meet at center, pressing to seal and form very small bun about 1½ inches in diameter and ½ inch high.

2. Place buns seam side down on ungreased baking sheet. Bake 11 to 14 minutes or until golden brown. Remove to wire racks.

3. Meanwhile, prepare burgers. Gently mix ground beef and seasoning mix in large bowl. Shape beef mixture into 36 patties, using about 2 teaspoons beef per patty.

4. Heat large skillet over medium heat 30 seconds. Place half of patties in skillet; cook 4 minutes on one side or until browned. Turn and cook 3 minutes or until burgers are cooked through; top with slice of cheese, if desired. Repeat with remaining patties.

5. To assemble, split buns in half crosswise. Top bottom halves with burgers, pickle slices, ketchup or mustard and tops of buns.

Makes 36 mini burgers

 ## Helpful Hint

When making burgers or meatballs,
it's important to use beef that is
not too lean—the lower the fat content of the beef,
the drier it will be after cooking. Choose ground
round (20 to 23 percent fat) or ground chuck
(23 to 30 percent fat) for the best results.

One-Bite Burgers

Hot & Sweet Deviled Eggs

6 hard-cooked eggs, peeled and cut lengthwise into halves
4 to 5 tablespoons mayonnaise
¼ teaspoon curry powder
¼ teaspoon black pepper
⅛ teaspoon salt
   Dash of paprika
¼ cup dried cherries or cranberries, finely chopped
1 teaspoon minced fresh chives
   Additional minced fresh chives (optional)

1. Scoop egg yolks into bowl; reserve whites. Mash yolks with mayonnaise until creamy. Stir in curry powder, pepper, salt and paprika; mix well. Stir in cherries and chives.

2. Spoon or pipe egg yolk mixture into egg whites. Garnish with additional chives. *Makes 12 servings*

Italian Stuffed Mushrooms

12 large mushrooms
½ pound sweet Italian sausage links, removed from casing
1 shallot, finely chopped or ¼ cup chopped onion
½ cup WISH-BONE® 5 Cheese Italian Dressing
2 tablespoons chopped drained sun-dried tomatoes packed in oil
¾ cup plain dry bread crumbs

1. Preheat oven to 400°F. Remove and finely chop mushroom stems to equal 1 cup; set aside.

2. In 12-inch nonstick skillet, brown sausage over medium-high heat, stirring frequently. Stir in chopped mushroom stems and shallot and cook, stirring occasionally, 4 minutes or until tender. Remove from heat. Stir in Wish-Bone 5 Cheese Italian Dressing, tomatoes and bread crumbs. Evenly spoon mixture into mushroom caps.

3. On baking sheet, arrange mushroom caps. Bake 25 minutes or until heated through and lightly browned. *Makes 12 appetizers*

Hot & Sweet Deviled Eggs

Chicken Meatballs with Chipotle-Honey Sauce

2 pounds ground chicken
2 eggs, lightly beaten
⅓ cup plain dry bread crumbs
⅓ cup chopped fresh cilantro
2 tablespoons fresh lime juice
4 cloves garlic, minced
1 can (4 ounces) chipotle peppers in adobo sauce, divided
1 teaspoon salt
   Chipotle-Honey Sauce (recipe follows)
2 tablespoons vegetable oil

1. Line two baking sheets with parchment paper. Combine chicken, eggs, bread crumbs, cilantro, lime juice, garlic, 1 tablespoon adobo sauce and salt in medium bowl; mix well. Form mixture into 48 meatballs. Place meatballs on prepared baking sheets. Cover with plastic wrap; chill 1 hour.

2. Prepare Chipotle-Honey sauce. Preheat oven to 400°F. Lightly brush meatballs with oil. Bake 12 minutes.

3. Transfer meatballs to baking dish. Add Chipotle-Honey Sauce; stir until coated. Bake 10 minutes or until meatballs are heated through and glazed with sauce. *Makes about 8 servings*

Chipotle-Honey Sauce

 ¾ cup honey
 2 to 3 whole chipotle peppers in adobo sauce
⅓ cup chicken broth
⅓ cup tomato paste
 1 tablespoon lime juice
 2 teaspoons Dijon mustard
½ teaspoon salt

Combine all ingredients in food processor or blender; process until smooth.
Makes about 1½ cups

Chicken Meatballs with Chipotle-Honey Sauce

Mexican Tortilla Stacks

½ cup ORTEGA® Salsa, any variety, divided
½ cup finely chopped cooked chicken
¼ cup sour cream
 8 (8-inch) ORTEGA Soft Flour Tortillas
½ cup prepared guacamole
⅓ cup ORTEGA Refried Beans
 6 tablespoons (1½ ounces) shredded Cheddar cheese
   Sour cream and chopped cilantro (optional)

HEAT oven to 350°F. Mix ¼ cup salsa, chicken and sour cream in small bowl.

PLACE 2 tortillas on ungreased cookie sheet; spread with salsa-chicken mixture. Spread 2 more tortillas with guacamole and place on top of salsa-chicken mixture.

MIX refried beans with remaining ¼ cup salsa; spread onto 2 more tortillas and place on top of guacamole. Top each stack with remaining 2 tortillas; sprinkle with cheese.

BAKE 8 to 10 minutes until cheese is melted and filling is hot.

TOP with sour cream and cilantro, if desired. Cut each stack into 8 wedges.

Makes 16 servings

Note: Prepared guacamole can be found in the refrigerated or frozen food sections at most supermarkets.

Mexican Tortilla Stacks

Mini Swiss Quiches

4 eggs
¼ teaspoon salt
¼ teaspoon black pepper
¾ cup (3 ounces) shredded Swiss cheese
1 unbaked 9-inch pie crust

1. Preheat oven to 300°F. Spray 20 mini (1¾-inch) muffin cups with nonstick cooking spray.

2. Whisk eggs, salt and pepper in medium bowl; stir in cheese.

3. Roll out pie crust dough to 13-inch circle. Cut dough with 3-inch round biscuit cutter. Gather and reroll scraps to make total of 20 circles. Press circles into prepared muffin cups. Fill cups with egg mixture.

4. Bake 30 minutes or until tops are puffy and toothpick inserted into centers comes out clean. *Makes 20 quiches*

Mini Asparagus Quiches

8 stalks asparagus
3 eggs
¼ teaspoon salt
¼ teaspoon black pepper
1 unbaked 9-inch pie crust

1. Preheat oven to 300°F. Spray 20 mini (1¾-inch) muffin cups with nonstick cooking spray.

2. Trim asparagus; thinly slice on the diagonal or coarsely chop. (This should be ½ cup.) Bring 3 cups water to a boil in medium saucepan. Add asparagus; cook 2 minutes over medium heat. Drain in colander; rinse under cold water to stop cooking.

3. Whisk eggs, salt and pepper in medium bowl; stir in asparagus.

4. Roll out pie crust dough to 13-inch circle. Cut dough with 3-inch round biscuit cutter. Gather and reroll scraps to make total of 20 circles. Press circles into prepared muffin cups. Fill cups with egg mixture.

5. Bake 30 minutes or until tops are lightly browned and toothpick inserted into centers comes out clean. *Makes 20 quiches*

*Mini Swiss Quiches and
Mini Asparagus Quiches*

Zesty Crab Cakes with Red Pepper Sauce

½ **pound raw medium shrimp, shelled and deveined**
⅔ **cup heavy cream**
 1 **egg white**
 3 **tablespoons** *Frank's® RedHot® Original Cayenne Pepper Sauce*
 1 **tablespoon** *French's® Worcestershire Sauce*
¼ **teaspoon seasoned salt**
 1 **pound crabmeat or imitation crabmeat, flaked (4 cups)**
 1 **red or yellow bell pepper, minced**
 2 **green onions, minced**
¼ **cup minced fresh parsley**
1½ **cups fresh bread crumbs**
½ **cup corn oil**
   Red Pepper Sauce (recipe follows)

1. Place shrimp, cream, egg white, **Frank's RedHot** Sauce, Worcestershire and seasoned salt in food processor. Process until mixture is puréed. Transfer to large bowl.

2. Add crabmeat, bell pepper, onions and parsley. Mix with fork until well blended.

3. Shape crabmeat mixture into 12 (½-inch-thick) patties, using about ¼ cup mixture for each. Coat both sides in bread crumbs.

4. Heat oil in large nonstick skillet. Add crab cakes; cook until browned on both sides. Drain on paper towels. Serve with Red Pepper Sauce.

Makes about 1 dozen crab cakes

Red Pepper Sauce: Place 1 jar (7 ounces) roasted red peppers, drained, ¼ cup mayonnaise, 3 tablespoons **Frank's RedHot** Sauce, 2 tablespoons minced onion, 1 tablespoon **French's** Spicy Brown Mustard, 1 tablespoon minced parsley and 1 clove garlic in blender or food processor. Cover; blend until smooth.

Prep Time: 30 minutes
Cook Time: 15 minutes

Zesty Crab Cakes with Red Pepper Sauce

Open-Faced Barbecue Chicken Sliders

1 pound (16 ounces) ground chicken
½ cup barbecue sauce, divided
4 slices sharp Cheddar cheese, cut into quarters
4 slices whole-wheat sandwich bread
Lettuce leaves

1. Combine chicken and ¼ cup barbecue sauce in medium bowl. Shape mixture into 16 meatballs.

2. Spray nonstick grill pan or large skillet with cooking spray; heat over medium-high heat. Place meatballs in pan; press with spatula to form patties. Cook 6 minutes per side or until patties are no longer pink in center. Top with cheese.

3. Meanwhile, cut bread slices into quarters or cut out circles with cookie cutter. Toast bread lightly. Top with lettuce and burgers; serve with remaining barbecue sauce. *Makes 16 burgers*

Baked Taco Chicken Bites

1 egg white, beaten
1 tablespoon water
¼ cup yellow cornmeal
2 tablespoons all-purpose flour
1 package (about 1 ounce) reduced-sodium taco seasoning
1 pound boneless skinless chicken breasts
2 tablespoons butter, melted
Ranch salad dressing or spicy ranch salad dressing

1. Preheat oven to 450°F. Grease baking sheet.

2. Combine egg white and water in shallow dish. Combine cornmeal, flour and taco seasoning in another shallow dish.

3. Cut chicken into 1½- to 2-inch pieces. Dip chicken pieces into egg white mixture; roll in cornmeal mixture to coat. Place in single layer on prepared baking sheet. Drizzle with melted butter. Bake 11 to 13 minutes or until chicken is no longer pink in center. Serve with salad dressing for dipping.
Makes 6 to 8 servings

Open-Faced Barbecue Chicken Sliders

Spanish Tortilla

1 tablespoon olive oil
1 cup thinly sliced peeled potato
1 small zucchini, thinly sliced
¼ cup chopped onion
1 clove garlic, minced
1 cup shredded cooked chicken
8 eggs
½ teaspoon salt
½ teaspoon black pepper
¼ teaspoon red pepper flakes
1 plum tomato, seeded and diced (optional)
Salsa (optional)

1. Heat oil in 10-inch nonstick skillet over medium-high heat. Add potato, zucchini, onion and garlic; cook and stir about 8 minutes or until potato is tender, turning frequently. Stir in chicken; cook 1 minute.

2. Meanwhile, whisk eggs, salt, pepper and red pepper flakes in large bowl. Carefully pour egg mixture into skillet. Reduce heat to low. Cover and cook 12 to 15 minutes or until egg mixture is set in center.

3. Loosen edges of tortilla and slide onto large serving platter. Let stand 5 minutes before cutting into wedges or 1-inch cubes. Serve warm or at room temperature. Garnish with diced tomato and serve with salsa, if desired. *Makes 10 to 12 servings*

 **Helpful Hint**

For a vegetarian dish, simply omit the chicken from the recipe. You can also substitute different vegetables for the zucchini—try spinach, chard or other greens in the tortilla (cook them in the skillet before adding the eggs).

Spanish Tortilla

Warm Goat Cheese Rounds

1 package (4 ounces) goat cheese
1 egg
1 tablespoon water
⅓ cup seasoned bread crumbs

1. Cut goat cheese log crosswise into eight ¼-inch slices. (If cheese is too difficult to slice, shape scant tablespoonfuls of goat cheese into balls and flatten into ¼-inch rounds.)

2. Beat egg and water in small bowl. Place bread crumbs in shallow dish. Dip goat cheese rounds into egg mixture, then in bread crumbs, turning to coat all sides. Gently press bread crumbs to adhere. Place coated rounds on plate; freeze 10 minutes.

3. Cook goat cheese rounds in medium nonstick skillet over medium-high heat about 2 minutes per side or until golden brown. Serve immediately.

Makes 4 servings

Serving Suggestions: Serve goat cheese rounds with heated marinara sauce or over mixed greens tossed with vinaigrette dressing.

Awesome Antipasto

1 jar (16 ounces) mild cherry peppers, drained
1 jar (9 ounces) artichoke hearts, drained
½ pound asparagus spears, cooked
½ cup pitted black olives
1 red onion, cut into thin wedges
1 green bell pepper, sliced into rings
1 red bell pepper, sliced into rings
1 bottle (8 ounces) Italian salad dressing
1 cup shredded Parmesan cheese, divided
1 package (6 ounces) HILLSHIRE FARM® Hard Salami

Layer cherry peppers, artichoke hearts, asparagus, olives, onion and bell peppers in 13×9-inch glass baking dish. Pour dressing and ⅓ cup cheese over vegetables. Cover; refrigerate 1 to 2 hours.

Drain vegetables, reserving marinade. Arrange vegetables and Hard Salami in rows on serving platter. Drizzle with reserved marinade. Top with remaining ⅔ cup cheese.

Makes 6 servings

Stuffed Mushroom Caps

2 packages (8 ounces each) whole mushrooms
1 tablespoon butter
⅔ cup finely chopped cooked chicken
¼ cup grated Parmesan cheese
1 tablespoon chopped fresh basil
2 teaspoons lemon juice
¼ teaspoon salt
⅛ teaspoon onion powder
   Pinch black pepper
1 small package (3 ounces) cream cheese, softened
   Paprika

1. Preheat oven to 350°F. Grease baking sheet. Remove stems from mushrooms; finely chop. Arrange mushroom caps on prepared baking sheet.

2. Melt butter in medium skillet over medium-high heat; cook chopped mushrooms 5 minutes. Add chicken, Parmesan cheese, basil, lemon juice, salt, onion powder and pepper; cook and stir 5 minutes. Remove from heat; stir in cream cheese. Spoon mixture into mushroom caps.

3. Bake 10 to 15 minutes or until heated through. Sprinkle with paprika.

Makes about 26 stuffed mushrooms

Southern Shrimp & Peach Kabobs

½ cup HELLMANN'S® or BEST FOODS® Real Mayonnaise
½ cup peach preserves
2 green onions, chopped
1 clove garlic, finely chopped
1 teaspoon hot pepper sauce
1 pound uncooked large shrimp, peeled and deveined
2 medium peaches, pitted and cut into wedges

1. In small bowl, combine Hellmann's or Best Foods Real Mayonnaise, preserves, green onions, garlic and hot pepper sauce. Reserve ½ cup mixture for dipping.

2. On skewers, alternately thread shrimp and peaches. Grill or broil kabobs, brushing with remaining mayonnaise mixture, turning once, 10 minutes or until shrimp turn pink. Serve with reserved dipping sauce.

Makes 4 servings

Mini Marinated Beef Skewers

1 boneless beef top sirloin (about 1 pound)
2 tablespoons dry sherry
2 tablespoons soy sauce
1 tablespoon dark sesame oil
2 cloves garlic, minced
18 cherry tomatoes

1. Cut beef crosswise into ⅛-inch slices. Place in large resealable food storage bag. Combine sherry, soy sauce, sesame oil and garlic in small bowl; pour over beef. Seal bag; turn to coat. Marinate in refrigerator at least 30 minutes or up to 2 hours. Soak 18 (6-inch) wooden skewers in water 20 minutes.

2. Preheat broiler. Drain beef; discard marinade. Weave beef accordion-style onto skewers. Place on rack of broiler pan.

3. Broil 4 to 5 inches from heat 4 minutes. Turn skewers over; broil 4 minutes or until beef is barely pink in center. Place 1 cherry tomato on each skewer. Serve warm or at room temperature.

Makes 18 appetizers

Cheesy Christmas Trees

½ cup mayonnaise
1 tablespoon dry ranch-style salad dressing mix
1 cup (4 ounces) shredded Cheddar cheese
¼ cup grated Parmesan cheese
12 slices firm white bread
¼ cup red bell pepper strips
¼ cup green bell pepper strips

1. Preheat broiler. Combine mayonnaise and salad dressing mix in medium bowl. Add cheeses; mix well.

2. Cut bread slices into Christmas tree shapes using cookie cutter. Spread about 1 tablespoon mayonnaise mixture over each tree. Decorate with bell pepper strips. Place on baking sheet.

3. Broil 4 inches from heat 2 to 3 minutes or until bubbling. Serve warm.

Makes about 12 appetizers

Mini Marinated Beef Skewers

Original Buffalo Chicken Wings

Zesty Blue Cheese Dip (recipe follows)
2½ pounds chicken wings, split and tips discarded
½ cup *Frank's® RedHot®* Original Cayenne Pepper Sauce (or to taste)
⅓ cup butter or margarine, melted
Celery sticks

1. Prepare Zesty Blue Cheese Dip.

2. Deep fry* wings at 400°F 12 minutes or until crisp and no longer pink; drain.

3. Combine *Frank's RedHot* Sauce and butter in large bowl. Add wings to sauce; toss well to coat evenly. Serve with Zesty Blue Cheese Dip and celery.   *Makes 24 to 30 individual pieces*

*Or, prepare wings using one of the cooking methods below. Add wings to sauce; toss well to coat evenly.

To Bake: Place wings in single layer on rack in foil-lined roasting pan. Bake at 425°F 1 hour or until crisp and no longer pink, turning once halfway through baking time.

To Broil: Place wings in single layer on rack in foil-lined roasting pan. Broil 6 inches from heat 15 to 20 minutes or until crisp and no longer pink, turning once halfway through cooking time.

To Grill: Place wings on oiled grid. Grill over medium heat 30 to 40 minutes or until crisp and no longer pink, turning often.

Zesty Blue Cheese Dip

½ cup blue cheese salad dressing
¼ cup sour cream
2 teaspoons *Frank's® RedHot®* Original Cayenne Pepper Sauce

Combine all ingredients in medium serving bowl; mix well. Garnish with crumbled blue cheese, if desired.   *Makes ¾ cup dip*

Original Buffalo Chicken Wings

Chili Puffs

1 package (about 17 ounces) frozen puff pastry, thawed
1 can (15 ounces) chili without beans
½ package (8 ounces) cream cheese, softened
½ cup (2 ounces) finely shredded sharp Cheddar cheese
  Sliced green onions (optional)

1. Preheat oven to 400°F. Roll each sheet of puff pastry into 18×9-inch rectangle on lightly floured surface. Cut each rectangle into 18 (3-inch) squares. Press dough into 36 mini (1¾-inch) muffin cups. Bake 10 minutes.

2. Combine chili and cream cheese in medium bowl until smooth. Fill each pastry shell with 2 teaspoons chili mixture, pressing down centers of pastry to fill, if necessary. Sprinkle evenly with Cheddar cheese.

3. Bake 5 to 7 minutes or until cheese is melted and edges of pastry are golden brown. Cool in pans 5 minutes. Remove from pans; garnish with green onions. *Makes 36 puffs*

Tip: Use a pizza cutter to easily cut puff pastry sheets into squares.

Pizza-Stuffed Mushrooms

12 large or 24 medium fresh mushrooms
¼ cup chopped green bell pepper
¼ cup chopped pepperoni or cooked, crumbled Italian sausage
1 cup (½ of 15-ounce can) CONTADINA® Pizza Sauce
½ cup (2 ounces) shredded mozzarella cheese

1. Wash and dry mushrooms; remove stems.

2. Chop ¼ cup stems. In small bowl, combine chopped stems, bell pepper, meat and pizza sauce.

3. Spoon mixture into mushroom caps; top with cheese.

4. Broil 6 to 8 inches from heat for 2 to 3 minutes or until cheese is melted and mushrooms are heated through.
Makes 12 large or 24 medium appetizers

Chili Puffs

Chipotle Chicken Quesadillas

1 package (8 ounces) cream cheese, softened
1 cup (4 ounces) shredded Mexican cheese blend
1 tablespoon minced chipotle pepper in adobo sauce
5 (10-inch) flour tortillas
5 cups shredded cooked chicken (about 1¼ pounds)
  Guacamole, sour cream, salsa and chopped fresh cilantro

1. Combine cheeses and pepper in large bowl.

2. Spread ⅓ cup cheese mixture over half of one tortilla. Top with about 1 cup chicken. Fold over tortilla. Repeat with remaining tortillas.

3. Heat large nonstick skillet over medium-high heat. Spray outside of each tortilla with nonstick cooking spray. Cook tortillas 2 to 3 minutes per side or until lightly browned.

4. Cut each tortilla into 4 wedges. Serve with guacamole, sour cream, salsa and cilantro. *Makes 5 servings*

Tip: Chipotle peppers in adobo sauce can be found in small cans in the Mexican food section of the supermarket.

Chili-Rubbed Shrimp

  2 teaspoons chili powder
1½ teaspoons ground cumin
  1 teaspoon garlic powder
  1 teaspoon hot paprika
  ½ teaspoon salt
 12 jumbo raw shrimp, peeled and deveined (with tails on)
  ⅓ cup olive oil
    Lemon wedges

1. Combine chili powder, cumin, garlic powder, paprika and salt in shallow bowl. Pat onto shrimp.

2. Heat oil in large skillet over medium-high heat. Add shrimp; cook 1 to 2 minutes per side or until shrimp are pink and opaque. Serve with lemon wedges. *Makes 4 servings*

Chipotle Chicken Quesadillas

Holiday Express

Croque Monsieur Bites

8 thin slices firm sandwich bread
4 slices Swiss cheese (about 4 ounces), halved
4 slices smoked ham (about 4 ounces)
   Dash grated nutmeg
2 tablespoons butter, melted

1. Cut crusts from bread. Place 4 bread slices on work surface. Layer each with cheese slice, ham slice, cheese slice and sprinkle of nutmeg. Top with remaining bread slices. Brush outside of sandwiches with melted butter.

2. Cook sandwiches in large skillet over medium heat 2 to 3 minutes per side or until golden brown and cheese is melted. Cut into quarters.

Makes 16 pieces

Tip: Sandwiches can be prepared ahead of time and reheated for an easy party appetizer. Leave sandwiches whole after cooking and refrigerate until ready to serve. Cut into quarters and place on foil-lined baking sheet; bake in preheated 350°F oven about 8 minutes or until sandwiches are heated through and cheese is melted.

Clockwise from top left: Croque Monsieur Bites, Pesto Scallop Skewers (page 84), Speedy Salami Spirals (page 82) and Ham & Cheese Snacks (page 86)

Smokey Chipotle Party Dip

¾ **cup sour cream**
¾ **cup mayonnaise**
¾ **cup ORTEGA® Salsa, any variety**
1 **package (1.25 ounces) ORTEGA Chipotle Taco Seasoning Mix**
   Chopped tomatoes, chopped cilantro, chopped ripe olives and shredded cheddar cheese
   Blue corn tortilla chips

COMBINE sour cream, mayonnaise, salsa and seasoning mix; stir until blended.

SPREAD dip in shallow serving dish or pie plate and sprinkle with tomatoes, cilantro, olives and cheese. Serve with tortilla chips.

Makes 2¼ cups dip

Tip: This flavorful dip is ready to go as soon as you make it, but can also be prepared and refrigerated up to 2 days before serving.

Sweet & Sour Shrimp Skewers

½ **pound medium raw shrimp, peeled and deveined (with tails on)**
1 **can (8 ounces) pineapple chunks in juice, drained**
¼ **cup sweet and sour sauce**

1. Alternately thread shrimp and pineapple chunks onto wooden skewers. Brush with sweet and sour sauce.

2. Heat large nonstick grill pan over medium-high heat. Cook skewers 3 minutes per side or until shrimp are pink and opaque. Serve with additional sweet and sour sauce for dipping, if desired.

Makes 10 to 12 servings

Smokey Chipotle Party Dip

Holiday Appetizer Puffs

1 sheet frozen puff pastry, thawed (half of 17-ounce package)
2 tablespoons olive or vegetable oil
   Toppings: grated Parmesan cheese, sesame seeds, poppy seeds,
      dried dill weed, dried basil, paprika, drained capers or
      pimiento-stuffed green olive slices

1. Preheat oven to 425°F. Roll out pastry on lightly floured surface into 13-inch square. Cut out shapes with cookie cutters. (Simple shapes work best.) Place on ungreased baking sheets. Brush cutouts lightly with oil; sprinkle with desired toppings.

2. Bake 6 to 8 minutes or until golden. Serve warm or at room temperature.

Makes about 1½ dozen appetizers

Cheesy Pizza Swirls

1 package (about 14 ounces) refrigerated pizza dough
⅓ cup prepared pizza sauce
1 cup (4 ounces) shredded pizza cheese

1. Preheat oven to 400°F. Line baking sheets with parchment paper.

2. Unroll dough on cutting board or clean work surface; press into 15×10-inch rectangle. Spread pizza sauce evenly over dough, leaving ½-inch border around edges. Sprinkle with cheese.

3. Starting with long side, tightly roll up dough and filling jelly-roll style, pinching seam to seal. Cut roll crosswise into ½-inch slices; arrange slices cut side down on prepared baking sheets. (If roll is too soft to cut, refrigerate or freeze until firm.)

4. Bake about 14 minutes or until golden brown.

Makes about 28 swirls

Pepperoni Pizza Swirls: Sprinkle ¼ cup chopped pepperoni over cheese before rolling up dough. Proceed as directed above.

Holiday Appetizer Puffs

Baked Brie

½ pound Brie cheese, rind removed
¼ cup chopped pecans
¼ cup KARO® Dark Corn Syrup

1. Preheat oven to 350°F. Place cheese in shallow oven-safe serving dish. Top with pecans and corn syrup.

2. Bake 8 to 10 minutes or until cheese is almost melted. Serve warm with plain crackers or Melba toast. *Makes 8 servings*

Prep Time: 3 minutes
Cook Time: 10 minutes

Crispy Ranch Chicken Bites

1 pound boneless skinless chicken breasts
¾ cup ranch dressing
2 cups panko bread crumbs

1. Preheat oven to 375°F. Line baking sheets with foil; spray foil with olive oil cooking spray.

2. Cut chicken into 1-inch cubes. Place ranch dressing in small bowl. Spread panko in shallow dish. Dip chicken in ranch dressing; tap off excess. Transfer chicken to panko; toss to coat, pressing panko into chicken. Place chicken on prepared baking sheets.

3. Spray breaded chicken with cooking spray. Bake 15 to 17 minutes or until golden brown, turning once. *Makes 6 to 8 servings*

Baked Brie

Spicy Marinated Shrimp

1 green onion, finely chopped
2 tablespoons olive oil
2 tablespoons fresh lemon juice
2 tablespoons prepared horseradish
2 tablespoons ketchup
1 tablespoon finely chopped chives
1 teaspoon Original TABASCO® brand Pepper Sauce
1 teaspoon Dijon mustard
1 clove garlic, minced
Salt to taste
2 pounds medium shrimp, cooked, peeled and deveined

Combine all ingredients except shrimp in large bowl. Add shrimp and toss to coat. Cover and refrigerate 4 to 6 hours or overnight. Transfer shrimp mixture to serving bowl and serve with toothpicks.

Makes 30 to 40 shrimp

Piquant Pepper Quesadillas

2 to 4 teaspoons vegetable oil
4 (10-inch) flour tortillas
4 cups (16 ounces) shredded Mexican cheese blend
1 cup chopped peppadew peppers or roasted red peppers
Sour cream, salsa and guacamole

1. Heat 1 teaspoon oil in large skillet over medium-high heat.

2. Place 1 tortilla in skillet; sprinkle ½ cup cheese and ¼ cup peppers over half of tortilla. Fold over tortilla. Cook 2 minutes per side or until cheese is melted and tortilla is lightly browned. Remove from skillet; cut into 4 or 5 wedges.

3. Repeat with remaining ingredients, adding more oil to skillet as needed. Serve with sour cream, salsa and guacamole.   *Makes 16 to 20 wedges*

Spicy Marinated Shrimp

Elegant Appetizer Bites

1 package (8 ounces) cream cheese, softened
2 ounces feta cheese with basil and tomato
2 cloves garlic, minced
30 mini phyllo shells (two 2.1-ounce packages) *or* 15 mini puff pastry
    shells
    Prepared toppings, such as sun-dried tomato pesto, red pepper and
    artichoke tapenade, basil pesto and/or black olive spread

1. Beat cream cheese, feta and garlic in small bowl with electric mixer at
low speed until well blended.

2. Spoon about 1½ teaspoons cheese mixture into each shell. Top with
½ teaspoon desired topping.   *Makes 30 appetizers*

Tip: To soften cream cheese quickly, remove wrapper and microwave on
HIGH 15 to 20 seconds.

Alouette® Cranberry Brie

1 (13.2 ounce) wheel ALOUETTE® Baby Brie®, Original
1 cup OCEAN SPRAY® Cran-Fruit Cranberry Orange
2 tablespoons packed dark brown sugar
3 teaspoons rum or orange extract
⅛ teaspoon ground nutmeg
2 tablespoons chopped pecans

Preheat oven at 450°F. Remove top rind of Alouette® Baby Brie® leaving
3-inch rim around circumference of cheese. In small bowl combine
Cran-Fruit, brown sugar, extract and nutmeg. Top Alouette® Baby Brie®
with cranberry mixture and sprinkle with pecans. Place in ovenproof dish
and bake for 4 to 5 minutes.

Serve warm with assorted crackers or apple slices.   *Makes 10 servings*

Elegant Appetizer Bites

Perfect Party Spinach Dip

1 envelope LIPTON® RECIPE SECRETS® Vegetable Soup Mix*
1 container (8 ounces) regular or light sour cream
1 cup HELLMANN'S® or BEST FOODS® Real Mayonnaise
1 package (10 ounces) frozen chopped spinach, thawed and
squeezed dry
1 can (8 ounces) water chestnuts, drained and chopped (optional)

*Also terrific with LIPTON® RECIPE SECRETS® Savory Herb with Garlic Soup Mix.

1. In medium bowl, combine all ingredients; chill at least 2 hours.

2. Serve with your favorite dippers.   *Makes 3 cups dip*

Speedy Salami Spirals

1 package (about 14 ounces) refrigerated pizza dough
1 cup (4 ounces) shredded Italian cheese blend
3 to 4 ounces thinly sliced Genoa salami

1. Preheat oven to 400°F. Line large baking sheet with parchment paper or spray with nonstick cooking spray.

2. Unroll dough on cutting board or clean work surface; press into 15×10-inch rectangle. Sprinkle evenly with cheese; top with salami.

3. Starting with long side, tightly roll up dough and filling jelly-roll style, pinching seam to seal. Cut roll crosswise into ½-inch slices; arrange slices cut side down on prepared baking sheet. (If roll is too soft to cut, refrigerate or freeze until firm.)

4. Bake about 15 minutes or until golden brown. Serve warm.

Makes about 28 spirals

Perfect Party Spinach Dip

Pesto Scallop Skewers

2 red or yellow bell peppers, cut into 1-inch pieces
16 jumbo sea scallops (about 1 pound)
2 tablespoons pesto

1. Thread two bell pepper pieces and one scallop onto each of 16 short bamboo skewers. Brush pesto over peppers and scallops.

2. Heat nonstick grill pan or large nonstick skillet over medium-high heat. Cook skewers 2 to 3 minutes per side or until scallops are opaque in center.

Makes 16 appetizers

Italian Sub Crostini

1 small loaf French bread (about 6 inches)
Olive oil
1 ball (8 ounces) fresh mozzarella cheese
8 ounces sliced prosciutto

1. Preheat oven to 400°F. Cut bread into ½-inch slices; brush with olive oil. Place slices on ungreased baking sheet. Bake 5 to 10 minutes or until crisp.

2. Cut mozzarella into 12 slices. Place one cheese slice on each bread slice.

3. Fold prosciutto in thirds lengthwise; cut crosswise into thin slices. Sprinkle over cheese.

4. Bake 2 to 3 minutes or until cheese melts. Serve immediately.

Makes 12 crostini

Tip: For an added layer of flavor, top the cheese with a basil leaf before sprinkling with prosciutto.

Pesto Scallop Skewers

Ham & Cheese Snacks

8 thin slices ham (about 6 ounces total)
2 tablespoons honey mustard
8 thin slices Meunster cheese (about 4 ounces total)
   Thin pretzel crisps or favorite crackers

1. Spread each ham slice with about ¾ teaspoon mustard. Top 1 ham slice with 1 cheese slice; top with second ham and cheese slices to create two double ham and cheese stacks.

2. Starting with long side, roll up each ham and cheese stack into spiral. Wrap tightly in plastic wrap; refrigerate 30 minutes or up to 24 hours.

3. Cut each ham roll into ½-inch slices. Serve on pretzel crisps.

Makes 4 servings

Baked Vidalia Onion Dip

1 cup chopped Vidalia onion
1 cup grated Parmesan cheese or shredded Swiss cheese
   (about 4 ounces)
1 cup HELLMANN'S® or BEST FOODS® Real Mayonnaise
1 clove garlic, finely chopped (optional)
   Hot pepper sauce to taste (optional)

1. Preheat oven to 375°F.

2. In 1-quart casserole, combine all ingredients. Bake uncovered 25 minutes or until golden brown. Serve with your favorite dippers.

Makes 2 cups dip

Prep Time: 10 minutes
Cook Time: 25 minutes

Ham & Cheese Snacks

Salmon Appetizers

1 package frozen puff pastry sheets, thawed
4 ounces smoked salmon, flaked
8 ounces cream cheese, softened
2 tablespoons snipped fresh chives
1½ teaspoons lemon juice

Preheat oven to 375°F. Cut twelve 2-inch rounds of dough from pastry sheet; place in greased muffin cups. (Freeze remaining pastry sheet for later use.) Top dough rounds with salmon. Mix cream cheese, chives and lemon juice until creamy. Top salmon with about 1 tablespoon cream cheese mixture or pipe cream cheese over salmon, if desired. Bake 15 to 18 minutes. Serve warm. *Makes 12 appetizers*

Favorite recipe from **Wisconsin Milk Marketing Board**

Maple-Orange Bites

1 (12-ounce) package JENNIE-O TURKEY STORE®
   Turkey Wieners
⅔ cup orange juice
¼ cup maple-flavored syrup
1 tablespoon cornstarch
1 tablespoon butter or margarine

Cut wieners into 1-inch pieces. In medium saucepan over medium heat, stir together orange juice, syrup and cornstarch. Cook and stir until mixture is thickened and bubbly. Stir in butter until melted. Stir in wieners. Cook about 5 minutes or until heated through. Serve warm with wooden picks. *Makes 24 servings*

Salmon Appetizers

Quick Cheese Log

1 container (8 ounces) chive and onion cream cheese, softened
1 cup (4 ounces) shredded Cheddar cheese
⅓ cup chopped walnuts

1. Combine cream cheese and Cheddar cheese in medium bowl; mix well. Shape cheese mixture into 5-inch-long roll.

2. Spread nuts on 12-inch square of foil. Place log on nuts and carefully roll to coat with nuts. Place on serving plate; serve immediately or wrap in foil and refrigerate up to 24 hours. Serve with crackers.

Makes 6 to 8 servings

Tip: For additional color and flavor, add chopped fresh parsley or basil to the chopped nuts before coating the cheese log with the mixture. Or, substitute chopped pecans or hazelnuts for the walnuts, if desired.

Sweet & Spicy Mini Franks

⅔ cup grape jelly
⅓ to ½ cup yellow mustard
1 package (1 pound) cocktail franks

1. Place jelly and mustard in medium saucepan. Heat over medium-low heat 5 minutes or just until jelly begins to melt; stir until well blended.

2. Add franks; cook 10 minutes or until franks are hot, stirring occasionally.

Makes 6 to 8 servings

Hot Pepper Cranberry Jelly Appetizer

½ **cup whole berry cranberry sauce**
¼ **cup apricot fruit spread**
1 **teaspoon sugar**
1 **teaspoon cider vinegar**
½ **teaspoon red pepper flakes**
½ **teaspoon grated fresh ginger**
  Assorted crackers and sliced cheeses

1. Combine cranberry sauce, fruit spread, sugar, vinegar and red pepper flakes in small saucepan. Cook over medium heat until sugar has dissolved. *Do not boil.* Transfer to bowl; cool completely. Stir in ginger.

2. To serve, top crackers with cheese slices and spoonful of cranberry mixture. *Makes 16 servings*

Tangy Wisconsin Blue Cheese Whip

1 **cup whipping cream**
½ **cup finely crumbled Wisconsin Blue cheese (2 ounces)**
1 **teaspoon dried basil, crushed**
¼ **teaspoon garlic salt**
½ **cup almonds, toasted and chopped**
  Assorted vegetable or fruit dippers

In a small mixer bowl combine whipping cream, Blue cheese, basil and garlic salt. Beat with an electric mixer on medium speed until slightly thickened. Gently fold in chopped almonds. Serve with vegetable or fruit dippers. (Dip can be made ahead and chilled, covered, up to 2 hours.)
Makes about 2 cups

Prep Time: 15 minutes

Favorite recipe from **Wisconsin Milk Marketing Board**

Hot Pepper Cranberry Jelly Appetizer

Festive Finger Foods

Smoked Salmon Omelet Roll-Ups

4 eggs
⅛ teaspoon black pepper
¼ cup chive and onion cream cheese, softened
1 package (about 4 ounces) smoked salmon, cut into bite-size pieces

1. Beat eggs and pepper in small bowl until very well blended (no streaks of white showing). Spray large (10- or 12-inch) nonstick skillet with nonstick cooking spray; heat over medium-high heat.

2. Pour half of egg mixture into skillet; tilt skillet to completely coat bottom with thin layer of eggs. Cook, without stirring, 2 to 4 minutes or until eggs are set. (Cooking time will vary depending on size of skillet.) Use spatula to carefully loosen omelet from skillet; slide onto cutting board. Repeat with remaining egg mixture to make second omelet.

3. Spread 2 tablespoons cream cheese over each omelet; top with smoked salmon pieces. Roll up omelets tightly; wrap in plastic wrap and refrigerate at least 30 minutes. Cut off ends, then cut omelet rolls crosswise into ½-inch slices. *Makes about 24 pieces*

Clockwise from top left: Smoked Salmon Omelet Roll-Ups, Turkey Canapés (page 102), Prosciutto & Asiago Garlands (page 120) and Chorizo & Caramelized Onion Tortilla (page 124)

94

Empanaditas

Chicken Filling (recipe follows)
Pastry for double crust 9-inch pie
1 egg yolk mixed with 1 teaspoon water

1. Preheat oven to 375°F. Prepare Chicken Filling.

2. Roll out pastry, half at a time, on floured surface to ⅛-inch thickness; cut into 2½-inch circles. Place about 1 teaspoon Chicken Filling on each circle. Fold dough over to make half moons; seal edges with fork. Prick tops; brush with egg mixture.

3. Place on ungreased baking sheets. Bake 12 to 15 minutes or until golden brown. Serve warm. *Makes about 3 dozen empanaditas*

Chicken Filling

1 tablespoon butter
1 cup finely chopped onion
2 cups finely chopped cooked chicken
¼ cup canned diced green chiles
1 tablespoon capers, rinsed, drained and coarsely chopped
¼ teaspoon salt
1 cup (4 ounces) shredded Monterey Jack cheese

Melt butter in medium skillet over medium heat. Add onion; cook until tender. Stir in chicken, chiles, capers and salt; cook 1 minute. Remove from heat and let cool; stir in cheese. *Makes about 3 cups filling*

Empanaditas

Two-Tomato Kalamata Crostini

 8 sun-dried tomatoes (not packed in oil)
 4 ounces baguette, cut into 20 (¼-inch-thick) slices
 5 ounces grape tomatoes, chopped
12 kalamata olives, pitted and chopped
 1 tablespoon extra-virgin olive oil
 2 teaspoons cider vinegar
1½ teaspoons dried basil
 ¼ teaspoon salt
 1 clove garlic, halved crosswise

1. Preheat oven to 350°F. Place sun-dried tomatoes in small bowl; cover with boiling water. Let stand 10 minutes. Drain; chop tomatoes.

2. Place bread slices on large baking sheet. Bake 10 minutes or until golden brown around edges. Cool on wire rack.

3. Meanwhile, combine grape tomatoes, sun-dried tomatoes, olives, oil, vinegar, basil and salt in medium bowl; mix well.

4. Rub bread slices with garlic. Top each bread slice with 1 tablespoon tomato mixture. *Makes 20 crostini*

Tip: Use a serrated knife to slice bread and tomatoes.

 Helpful Hint

Kalamata olives are plump and juicy, with a dark purple color and rich, fruity flavor. They are often slit so that the wine vinegar marinade that they soak in can be absorbed. They are typically sold in jars, packed in either olive oil or vinegar.

Two-Tomato Kalamata Crostini

Chile 'n' Cheese Spirals

4 ounces cream cheese, softened
1 cup (4 ounces) shredded cheddar cheese
1 can (4 ounces) ORTEGA® Diced Green Chiles
3 green onions, sliced
½ cup chopped red bell pepper
1 can (2.25 ounces) chopped ripe olives
4 (8-inch) taco-size flour tortillas
ORTEGA Salsa, any variety

COMBINE cream cheese, cheddar cheese, chiles, green onions, pepper and olives in medium bowl.

SPREAD ½ cup cheese mixture on each tortilla; roll up. Wrap each roll in plastic wrap; chill for 1 hour.

REMOVE plastic wrap; slice each roll into six ¾-inch pieces. Serve with salsa for dipping. *Makes 24 appetizers*

Tip: Chile 'n' Cheese Spirals can be prepared and kept in the refrigerator for 1 to 2 days.

Sausage Pinwheels

2 cups biscuit mix
½ cup milk
¼ cup butter or margarine, melted
1 pound BOB EVANS® Original Recipe Roll Sausage

Combine biscuit mix, milk and butter in large bowl until blended. Refrigerate 30 minutes. Divide dough into two portions. Roll out one portion on floured surface to ⅛-inch-thick rectangle, about 10×7 inches. Spread with half the sausage. Roll lengthwise into long roll. Repeat with remaining dough and sausage. Place rolls in freezer until firm enough to cut easily. Preheat oven to 400°F. Cut rolls into thin slices. Place on *ungreased* baking sheets. Bake 15 minutes or until golden brown. Serve hot. Refrigerate leftovers. *Makes 48 pinwheels*

Note: This recipe can be doubled. Refreeze after slicing. When ready to serve, thaw slices in refrigerator and bake.

Chile 'n' Cheese Spirals

Mediterranean Flatbread

   2 tablespoons olive oil, divided
   ½ cup thinly sliced yellow onion
   ½ cup thinly sliced red bell pepper
   ½ cup thinly sliced green bell pepper
   1 package (11 ounces) refrigerated French bread dough
   2 cloves garlic, minced
   ½ teaspoon dried rosemary
   ⅛ teaspoon red pepper flakes (optional)
   ⅓ cup coarsely chopped pitted kalamata olives
   ¼ cup grated Parmesan cheese

1. Preheat oven to 350°F. Heat 1 tablespoon oil in large skillet over medium-high heat. Add onion and bell peppers; cook and stir 5 minutes or until onion begins to brown. Remove from heat.

2. Unroll dough on nonstick baking sheet. Combine garlic and remaining 1 tablespoon oil in small bowl; spread evenly over dough. Sprinkle with rosemary and red pepper flakes, if desired. Top with onion mixture; sprinkle with olives.

3. Bake 16 to 18 minutes or until golden brown. Sprinkle with Parmesan. Cool on wire rack. Cut flatbread in half lengthwise; cut crosswise into 1-inch-wide strips.   *Makes about 16 pieces*

Turkey Canapés

   8 slices JENNIE-O TURKEY STORE® Turkey Pastrami, Turkey Salami or Turkey Ham
   32 buttery round crackers, wheat crackers or rye crackers
   ¾ cup (6 ounces) cream cheese with chives or herb-flavored cream cheese
   1 small cucumber
   Fresh dill (optional)

Cut each slice of turkey into quarters; set aside. Spread each cracker with about 1 teaspoon cream cheese. Fold turkey quarters in half. Place turkey on cream cheese. Cut cucumber lengthwise in half; cut each half into ¼-inch slices. Top each cracker with cucumber slice and garnish with fresh dill, if desired.   *Makes 32 servings*

Mediterranean Flatbread

Alouette® Garlic and Herb Croustades

1 tablespoon olive oil
½ cup bacon, diced
1 cup baby bella or other mushrooms, chopped
⅔ cup chopped roasted red bell pepper
½ cup minced onion
1 teaspoon chopped garlic
1 (6.5-ounce) *or* 2 (4-ounce) packages ALOUETTE® Garlic & Herbs Spreadable Cheese
2 tablespoons fresh parsley or 1 tablespoon dried parsley flakes
2 (2-ounce) packages mini phyllo shells

In nonstick pan over medium heat, heat oil and sauté bacon for 3 to 5 minutes. Add mushrooms, pepper, onion and garlic; sauté for 3 to 5 minutes. Drain oil from pan; reduce heat to low and add Alouette®. Blend and simmer for 1 minute. Remove from heat; stir in parsley. Spoon 1 heaping teaspoon into each phyllo shell; serve warm.

Makes 30 appetizers

Tip: For a creative touch, use any variety of seasonally fresh vegetables, such as chopped fennel, summer or winter squash.

Roast Beef Roll-Ups

1 package (8 ounces) cream cheese, softened
1 cup (4 ounces) crumbled blue cheese
1 teaspoon Dijon mustard
½ teaspoon black pepper
1 pound sliced deli roast beef
1 small red onion, thinly sliced
12 butter lettuce leaves (about 1 head)

1. Mix cream cheese, blue cheese, mustard and pepper in small bowl until well blended.

2. Spread each slice of roast beef with 1 tablespoon cheese mixture. Top with 1 to 2 onion slices and 1 lettuce leaf. Roll up roast beef slices starting at short end; secure with toothpicks, if necessary. Cover and refrigerate until ready to serve. *Makes about 12 servings*

Alouette® Garlic and Herb Croustades

Tiny Spinach Quiches

Pastry
> 1 package (3 ounces) cream cheese, softened
> ½ cup (1 stick) butter or margarine, softened
> 1 cup all-purpose flour

Filling
> 5 slices bacon, cooked and crumbled
> 1 cup grated Swiss cheese
> 1 can (13.5 ounces) POPEYE® Chopped Spinach, drained
> 3 eggs
> ¾ cup light cream
> ¼ teaspoon ground nutmeg
> Salt and pepper to taste

1. To prepare pastry: Cut cream cheese and butter into flour. Form into a ball; wrap in plastic wrap and chill 1 hour. Lightly flour rolling pin. Place pastry on lightly floured work surface, roll out to ⅛-inch thickness and cut into 16 circles with 3-inch biscuit cutter. Line sixteen 1½-inch plain or fluted muffin pan cups, or mini-muffin pan cups, with dough circles.

2. To prepare filling: Preheat oven to 375°F. Sprinkle bacon, then cheese, evenly over bottoms of unbaked pastries. Squeeze spinach dry and spread evenly over bacon and cheese. In medium bowl, combine remaining ingredients. Pour evenly into pastry cups. Bake 30 minutes or until set.

Makes 16 appetizers

Note: To serve as a pie, pour filling into one 9-inch frozen ready-to-bake pie crust.

Tiny Spinach Quiches

Arugula-Prosciutto Wrapped Breadsticks with Garlic Mustard Sauce

½ **cup mayonnaise**
 6 **tablespoons grated Parmesan cheese**
 2 **tablespoons** *French's*® **Honey Dijon Mustard**
 1 **tablespoon chopped fresh basil**
 2 **teaspoons minced garlic**
 1 **package (4½ ounces) long breadsticks (12 to 16 breadsticks)**
 1⅓ **cups** *French's*® **French Fried Onions, crushed**
 ½ **pound thinly sliced prosciutto or smoked deli ham**
 1 **bunch arugula (about 20 leaves) or green leaf lettuce, washed, drained and stems removed**

1. Combine mayonnaise, cheese, mustard, basil and garlic in mixing bowl. Spread half of each breadstick with some of mustard sauce. Roll in French Fried Onions, pressing firmly.

2. Arrange prosciutto slices on flat work surface. Top each slice with leaf of arugula. Place coated end of breadsticks on top; roll up jelly-roll style. Place seam side down on serving platter.

3. Serve wrapped breadsticks with remaining mustard sauce for dipping.

Makes 16 appetizers

Prep Time: 25 minutes

 ### Helpful Hint

Arugula is an aromatic salad green with a peppery mustard flavor. Choose bunches with fresh looking, brightly colored leaves and store them tightly wrapped in a plastic bag in the refrigerator. They should be used within two days and washed very well just before using.

Arugula-Prosciutto Wrapped Breadsticks with Garlic Mustard Sauce

Caramelized Onion Focaccia

2 tablespoons plus 1 teaspoon olive oil, divided
4 medium onions, cut in half and thinly sliced
½ teaspoon salt
2 tablespoons water
1 tablespoon chopped fresh rosemary leaves
¼ teaspoon black pepper
1 loaf (16 ounces) frozen bread dough, thawed
1 cup (4 ounces) shredded fontina cheese
¼ cup grated Parmesan cheese

1. Heat 2 tablespoons oil in large skillet over high heat. Add onions and salt; cook about 10 minutes or until onions begin to brown, stirring occasionally. Stir in water. Reduce heat to medium; partially cover and cook about 20 minutes or until onions are deep golden brown, stirring occasionally. Remove from heat; stir in rosemary and pepper. Let cool slightly.

2. Meanwhile, brush 13×9-inch baking pan with remaining 1 teaspoon oil. Roll out dough to 13×9-inch rectangle on lightly floured surface. Transfer dough to prepared pan; cover and let rise in warm, draft-free place 30 minutes.

3. Preheat oven to 375°F. Prick dough all over (about 12 times) with fork. Sprinkle fontina cheese over dough; top with caramelized onions. Sprinkle with Parmesan cheese.

4. Bake 18 to 20 minutes or until golden brown. Remove from pan to wire rack. Cut into pieces; serve warm. *Makes 12 servings*

Caramelized Onion Focaccia

Margherita Panini Bites

1 loaf (16 ounces) ciabatta or crusty Italian bread, cut into
  16 (½-inch) slices
8 teaspoons prepared pesto
16 fresh basil leaves
8 slices mozzarella cheese
24 thin slices plum tomatoes (about 3 tomatoes)
  Olive oil

1. Preheat indoor grill. Spread each of 8 bread slices with 1 teaspoon pesto. Top each slice with 2 basil leaves, 1 cheese slice and 3 tomato slices. Top with remaining bread slices.

2. Brush both sides of sandwiches lightly with olive oil. Grill sandwiches 5 minutes or until lightly browned and cheese is melted.

3. Cut each sandwich into 4 pieces. Serve warm.   *Makes 32 panini bites*

Bacon-Wrapped Apricots

14 water chestnuts, drained
14 slices bacon
¼ cup packed brown sugar
½ teaspoon black pepper
28 Mediterranean dried apricots* (one 7-ounce package)

*Mediterranean dried apricots are plump, pitted whole dried apricots, available in the dried fruit section of most supermarkets.

1. Preheat oven to 425°F. Line shallow baking pan or baking sheet with parchment paper. Cut water chestnuts in half crosswise.

2. Place bacon slices on cutting board; cut in half crosswise. Sprinkle with brown sugar and pepper, pressing into bacon to adhere.

3. Fold apricot around water chestnut half. Wrap half slice bacon around each apricot; secure with toothpick.

4. Arrange apricots in prepared baking pan, spacing at least 1 inch apart. Bake about 20 minutes, turning after 10 minutes, or until bacon is cooked through.   *Makes 14 servings*

Margherita Panini Bites

Wisconsin Asiago Cheese Puffs

1 cup water
1 tablespoon butter
1 tablespoon olive oil
½ teaspoon salt
  Cayenne pepper to taste
1 cup flour
4 eggs*
½ cup (2 ounces) finely shredded Wisconsin Asiago cheese
½ cup (2 ounces) grated Wisconsin Parmesan cheese

*For lighter puffs, use 2 whole eggs and 4 egg whites.

Preheat oven to 400°F. In small saucepan, combine water, butter, oil, salt and cayenne; bring to a boil. Add flour all at once; stir until mixture forms a smooth ball. Cook over low heat until mixture is drier but still smooth; transfer mixture to large bowl. Beat in eggs, one at a time. Stir in cheeses. Drop batter by measuring tablespoonfuls onto greased cookie sheet. Bake for 20 minutes or until lightly browned and firm. Serve immediately.

Makes about 30 puffs

Favorite recipe from **Wisconsin Milk Marketing Board**

Shrimp Quesadillas

½ cup ricotta cheese
1 medium green onion, sliced
2 tablespoons TABASCO® brand Green Jalapeño Pepper Sauce, divided
4 (7-inch) flour tortillas
8 ounces shrimp, cooked and chopped
1 small tomato, chopped
½ cup (2 ounces) shredded Muenster cheese

Preheat oven to 450°F. Combine ricotta cheese, green onion and 1 tablespoon TABASCO® Green Sauce in small bowl. Spread on 2 tortillas; sprinkle with half of chopped shrimp. Top with remaining tortillas.

Top with remaining shrimp, tomato and Muenster cheese; sprinkle with remaining 1 tablespoon TABASCO® Green Sauce. Bake 5 to 8 minutes or until cheese is melted. Cut into wedges.   *Makes 4 appetizer servings*

Wisconsin Asiago Cheese Puffs

French-Style Pizza Bites

2 tablespoons olive oil
1 medium onion, thinly sliced
1 medium red bell pepper, cut into 3-inch-long strips
2 cloves garlic, minced
⅓ cup pitted black olives, cut into thin wedges
1 package (about 14 ounces) refrigerated pizza dough
¾ cup (3 ounces) finely shredded Swiss or Gruyère cheese

1. Position oven rack to lowest position. Preheat oven to 425°F. Grease large baking sheet.

2. Heat oil in medium skillet over medium heat. Add onion, bell pepper and garlic; cook and stir 5 minutes or until crisp-tender. Stir in olives. Remove from heat; set aside.

3. Pat dough into 16×12-inch rectangle on prepared baking sheet. Arrange onion mixture over dough; sprinkle with cheese. Bake 10 minutes. Loosen crust from baking sheet with long spatula. Slide crust onto oven rack. Bake 3 to 5 minutes more or until golden brown.

4. Slide baking sheet under crust; remove crust from rack. Transfer to cutting board. Cut pizza crosswise into eight 1¾-inch-wide strips. Cut pizza diagonally into ten 2-inch-wide strips, making diamond pieces. Serve immediately. *Makes about 24 pieces*

 ### Helpful Hint

The French-style pizza known as "pissaladière" is a specialty of Nice, a city in the south of France. The traditional recipe calls for a thin, pizza-like dough topped with onions, black olives and anchovies (no cheese).

French-Style Pizza Bites

Honey Holiday Wraps

1 package frozen puff pastry sheets, thawed according to package directions
1 egg, beaten
¼ cup Honey Mustard Sauce (recipe follows)
½ pound JENNIE-O TURKEY STORE® Deli Homestyle Honey Cured Turkey Breast, thinly sliced and finely diced
¼ cup walnuts, toasted and chopped
4 ounces Brie cheese, cut into 18 pieces

Preheat oven to 375°F. Remove pastry sheets from package and cut each into 9 smaller squares. Brush squares with egg and drizzle each with small amount of Honey Mustard Sauce. Toss diced JENNIE-O TURKEY STORE® Homestyle Honey Cured Turkey Breast with walnuts and then put about 1 teaspoon turkey mixture in center of each pastry square. Top with piece of Brie cheese; fold pastry over diagonally to form triangle, pressing edges to seal. Pinch together two corners on folded edge of pastry, and place tortellini shape on baking sheet. Bake at 375°F for 15 to 18 minutes. Allow to cool slightly before serving. Serve with additional Honey Mustard Sauce, if desired. *Makes 18 wraps*

Honey Mustard Sauce: Mix together 2 tablespoons Dijon mustard and 2 tablespoons honey. Makes ¼ cup.

Variations: Any variety of JENNIE-O TURKEY STORE® turkey or chicken breast can be used in this recipe. Try apple butter or pesto sauce instead of honey mustard.

Prep Time: 30 minutes
Cook Time: 15 to 18 minutes

Honey Holiday Wraps

Bell Pepper Wedges with Herbed Goat Cheese

2 small red bell peppers
1 log (4 ounces) plain goat cheese, at room temperature
⅓ cup whipped cream cheese
2 tablespoons minced fresh chives
1 teaspoon minced fresh dill
  Fresh dill sprigs (optional)

1. Cut off top quarter of bell peppers; remove core and seeds. Cut each pepper into 6 wedges. Remove ribs, if necessary.

2. Combine goat cheese, cream cheese, chives and dill in small bowl until well blended. Pipe or spread 1 tablespoon goat cheese mixture onto each pepper wedge. Garnish with dill sprigs.   *Makes 6 servings*

Prosciutto & Asiago Garlands

1 package (11 ounces) refrigerated breadstick dough
    (12 breadsticks)
6 slices prosciutto (one 4-ounce package)
½ to ¾ cup grated Asiago or Parmesan cheese
  Dijon mustard (optional)

1. Preheat oven to 375°F. Line large baking sheet with parchment paper.

2. Separate dough into 12 breadsticks. Cut each slice of prosciutto in half lengthwise. Place prosciutto strip over breadstick, adding prosciutto scraps to cover breadstick, if necessary. Twist tightly on both ends to wrap prosciutto in breadstick dough. Bring ends of dough together to form garland about 3 inches in diameter; press ends to seal.

3. Spread cheese in shallow dish. Lightly dip each garland in cheese to coat one side only. Place garlands, cheese side up, on prepared baking sheet.

4. Bake 15 minutes or until golden brown and cheese is melted. Serve with mustard for dipping, if desired.   *Makes 12 servings*

Bell Pepper Wedges with Herbed Goat Cheese

Roasted Red Potato Bites

1½ pounds red potatoes (about 15 small)
  1 cup shredded Cheddar cheese (about 4 ounces)
  ½ cup HELLMANN'S® or BEST FOODS® Real Mayonnaise
  ½ cup sliced green onions
  10 slices bacon, crisp-cooked and crumbled
  2 tablespoons chopped fresh basil leaves (optional)

1. Preheat oven to 400°F. On large baking sheet, arrange potatoes and bake 35 minutes or until tender. Let stand until cool enough to handle.

2. Cut each potato in half, then cut thin slice from bottom of each potato half. With small melon baller or spoon, scoop pulp from potatoes leaving ¼-inch shell. Place pulp in medium bowl; set shells aside.

3. Lightly mash pulp. Stir in remaining ingredients. Spoon or pipe potato filling into potato shells. Arrange filled shells on baking sheet and broil 3 minutes or until golden and heated through.   *Makes 30 bites*

Open-Faced Reubens

1 box (6 ounces) rye Melba toast rounds
  ¼ pound thinly sliced cooked corned beef, cut into ½-inch squares
  1 can (8 ounces) sauerkraut, rinsed, drained and chopped
  1 cup (4 ounces) finely shredded Wisconsin Swiss cheese
  2 teaspoons prepared mustard
    Caraway seeds

Preheat oven to 350°F. Arrange toast rounds on baking sheets. Top each with 1 beef square and 1 teaspoon sauerkraut. Combine cheese and mustard in small bowl; spoon about 1 teaspoon cheese mixture on top of sauerkraut. Sprinkle with caraway seeds. Bake about 5 minutes or until cheese is melted.   *Makes about 48 appetizer servings*

Microwave Directions: Arrange 8 toast rounds around edge of microwave-safe plate lined with paper towel. Place 2 rounds in center. Top as directed. Microwave, uncovered, on MEDIUM (50% power) 1 to 2 minutes until cheese is melted, turning plate once. Repeat with remaining ingredients.

*Favorite recipe from **Wisconsin Milk Marketing Board***

Roasted Red Potato Bites

Chorizo & Caramelized Onion Tortilla

¼ **cup olive oil**
3 **medium yellow onions, quartered and sliced**
½ **pound Spanish chorizo (about 2 links) or andouille sausage, diced**
6 **eggs**
   Salt and black pepper
½ **cup chopped fresh parsley**

1. Preheat oven to 350°F. Spray 9-inch square baking pan with olive oil cooking spray.

2. Heat oil in medium skillet over medium heat. Add onions; cover and cook 10 minutes or until onions are translucent. Reduce heat to low; cook, uncovered, 40 minutes or until golden and very tender. Remove onions from skillet; set aside to cool.

3. Add chorizo to same skillet. Cook over medium heat 5 minutes or until chorizo just begins to brown, stirring occasionally. Remove chorizo from skillet; set aside to cool.

4. Whisk eggs in medium bowl; season with salt and pepper. Add onions, chorizo and parsley; stir gently until well blended. Pour egg mixture into prepared pan. Bake 12 to 15 minutes or until center is almost set. *Turn oven to broil.* Broil 1 to 2 minutes or until top just starts to brown. Remove pan to wire rack; cool completely. Cut into 36 squares; serve cold or at room temperature. *Makes 36 squares*

Tip: The tortilla can be made up to 1 day ahead and refrigerated until ready to serve. To serve at room temperature, remove from refrigerator 30 minutes before serving.

Spinach-Artichoke Cheese Squares

1 box (11 ounces) pie crust mix
1 container (15 ounces) part-skim ricotta cheese
½ cup grated Parmesan cheese
4 eggs
¼ cup plain dry bread crumbs
¼ cup *French's*® Honey Dijon Mustard
1 teaspoon dried Italian seasoning
2 packages (10 ounces each) frozen chopped spinach, thawed and
    squeezed dry
1 jar (12 ounces) marinated artichoke hearts, drained and chopped
4 green onions, thinly sliced
½ cup chopped pimiento, well drained

1. Preheat oven to 400°F. Coat 15×10×1-inch baking pan with nonstick cooking spray. Toss pie crust mix with ⅓ cup cold water in large bowl until moistened and crumbly. Press mixture firmly onto bottom of prepared pan using floured bottom of measuring cup. Prick with fork. Bake 20 minutes or until golden.

2. Combine cheeses, eggs, bread crumbs, mustard and Italian seasoning in large bowl until well blended. Stir in vegetables; mix well. Spoon over baked crust, spreading evenly.

3. Bake 20 minutes or until toothpick inserted into center comes out clean. Cool on wire rack 15 minutes. Cut into squares. Serve warm or at room temperature. *Makes 24 servings*

Prep Time: 25 minutes
Bake Time: 40 minutes

Merry Munchies

Holiday Pizza Bites

  1 tablespoon olive oil
½ small onion, finely diced
⅛ teaspoon salt
½ small red bell pepper, finely diced
½ small green bell pepper, finely diced
    Pinch red pepper flakes (optional)
  1 package (about 14 ounces) refrigerated pizza dough
⅓ cup pizza sauce
½ cup shredded pizza cheese

1. Preheat oven to 425°F. Lightly grease large baking sheet.

2. Heat oil in medium skillet over medium-high heat. Add onion and salt; cook and stir 5 minutes. Add bell peppers and red pepper flakes; cook and stir 5 minutes or until tender. Let cool slightly.

3. Meanwhile, unroll dough on work surface; press into 12×8-inch rectangle. Cut out shapes with 2½- to 3½-inch metal holiday cookie cutters. Place shapes 1 inch apart on prepared baking sheet.

4. Bake about 7 minutes or until light golden brown. Remove from oven; spread scant 1 teaspoon pizza sauce over each crust. Sprinkle evenly with cheese; top with bell pepper mixture. Bake 3 to 5 minutes or until cheese is melted and lightly browned.   *Makes about 18 appetizers*

Clockwise from top left: Holiday Pizza Bites,
Easy Cheesy Artichoke & Spinach Bread
(page 128), Super Salami Twists (page 150) and
Sweet Onion & Pumpkin Seed Focaccia (page 136)

Spicy Roasted Chickpeas

1 can (about 20 ounces) chickpeas
3 tablespoons olive oil
½ teaspoon salt
½ teaspoon black pepper
¾ to 1 tablespoon chili powder
⅛ to ¼ teaspoon ground red pepper
1 lime, cut into wedges

1. Preheat oven to 400°F. Rinse chickpeas in colander; drain well, shaking colander to remove as much water as possible.

2. Combine chickpeas, olive oil, salt and black pepper in baking pan large enough to hold chickpeas in single layer. Bake 15 minutes or until chickpeas begin to brown, shaking pan twice during baking.

3. Sprinkle with chili powder and red pepper to taste; bake 5 minutes or until dark golden-red. Serve with lime wedges. *Makes 4 to 6 servings*

Easy Cheesy Artichoke & Spinach Bread

1 can (14 ounces) artichoke hearts, drained and chopped
1 package (10 ounces) frozen chopped spinach or chopped broccoli, thawed and squeezed dry
1 cup HELLMANN'S® or BEST FOODS® Real Mayonnaise
1 cup grated Parmesan cheese
1 clove garlic, finely chopped *or* ¼ teaspoon LAWRY'S® Garlic Powder with Parsley (optional)
1 loaf French or Italian bread (about 16 inches long), halved lengthwise

1. Preheat oven to 350°F.

2. In small bowl, combine all ingredients except bread; evenly spread on bread. Bake 12 minutes or until golden and heated through.

Makes 8 servings

Prep Time: 10 minutes
Cook Time: 12 minutes

Spicy Roasted Chickpeas

Ham & Swiss Twists

1 package (about 14 ounces) refrigerated pizza dough
6 very thin slices smoked ham
6 very thin slices Swiss cheese
  Black pepper

1. Preheat oven to 400°F. Line baking sheets with parchment paper.

2. Unroll dough on cutting board or clean work surface; press into 16×12-inch rectangle. Arrange single layer of cheese slices over half of dough, cutting slices to fit as necessary. Top with ham slices; sprinkle with pepper. Fold remaining half of dough over ham and cheese layers, creating 12×8-inch rectangle.

3. Cut dough into ½-inch strips (8 inches long). Twist strips several times; place on prepared baking sheets. Bake about 14 minutes or until golden brown. Serve warm. *Makes about 22 twists*

Tip: For extra flavor, spread honey or Dijon mustard over dough before layering with cheese and ham. Serve with additional mustard for dipping.

Note: Ham & Swiss Twists are about 10 to 12 inches long. For shorter twists, cut them in half after baking.

Parmesan-Sage Crisps

1½ cups (about 4 ounces) shredded Parmesan cheese*
2 to 3 tablespoons finely chopped fresh sage leaves
½ teaspoon black pepper

Purchase pre-shredded cheese for this recipe. Do not use finely grated cheese.

1. Preheat oven to 350°F. Line baking sheets with parchment paper.

2. Combine cheese, sage and pepper in medium bowl; mix well. Place scant ⅓ cup cheese mixture onto prepared baking sheet; spread into 5-inch circle. Repeat with remaining cheese mixture.

3. Bake 7 to 8 minutes or just until lightly browned. Cool on baking sheets about 2 minutes. When cool enough to handle, peel cheese crisps from paper. Cool completely. Cut or break into pieces. *Makes 8 servings*

Ham & Swiss Twists

Spicy Cocoa Glazed Pecans

¼ cup plus 2 tablespoons sugar, divided
1 cup warm water
1½ cups pecan halves or pieces
1 tablespoon HERSHEY'S Cocoa
3 to 4 teaspoons chili powder
⅛ to ¼ teaspoon cayenne pepper

1. Heat oven to 350°F. Lightly spray shallow baking pan with vegetable cooking spray.

2. Stir together ¼ cup sugar and warm water until sugar dissolves. Add pecans; let soak 10 minutes. Drain water and discard.

3. Stir together remaining 2 tablespoons sugar, cocoa, chili powder and cayenne pepper in medium bowl. Add pecans; toss until all cocoa mixture coats pecans. Spread coated pecans in prepared pan.

4. Bake 10 to 15 minutes or until pecans start to glisten and appear dry. Stir occasionally while baking. Cool completely. Store in cool, dry place. Serve as a snack with beverages or sprinkle in salads.

Makes 1½ cups coated pecans

Ortega® Nachos

1 can (16 ounces) ORTEGA® Refried Beans, heated
4 cups (4 ounces) tortilla chips
1½ cups (6 ounces) shredded Monterey Jack cheese
¼ cup ORTEGA Sliced Jalapeños
ORTEGA Salsa, any variety, sliced green onions, guacamole, sliced olives, chopped cilantro and sour cream (optional)

PREHEAT broiler.

SPREAD beans over bottom of large ovenproof platter or 15×10×1-inch jelly-roll pan. Arrange chips over beans. Top with cheese and jalapeños.

BROIL for 1 to 1½ minutes or until cheese is melted. Top with salsa, green onions and other garnishes, if desired. *Makes 4 to 6 servings*

Spicy Cocoa Glazed Pecans

Rosemary Wine Crackers

1 cup whole wheat flour
1 tablespoon chopped fresh rosemary leaves
⅛ teaspoon salt
3 tablespoons olive oil
¼ cup wine (preferably a fruity white or rosé)
Coarse salt (optional)

1. Preheat oven to 400°F. Line cookie sheet with parchment paper; dust paper lightly with flour.

2. Place flour, rosemary and salt in food processor; pulse 30 seconds to combine. With motor running, gradually add olive oil and wine. When mixture forms a ball on top of blade, stop adding wine. Remove dough to prepared cookie sheet.

3. Roll out dough as thin as possible (⅛ inch or less) on cookie sheet. Sprinkle with coarse salt, if desired, and roll lightly to press salt into dough. Score dough into squares or diamonds with knife or pizza cutter.

4. Bake 10 to 15 minutes or until crackers begin to brown around edges, rotating pan halfway through baking time. Remove to wire rack to cool completely. Break into individual crackers. Store in airtight container. To re-crisp, place in 350°F oven for 5 minutes.

Makes about 2 dozen crackers

Helpful Hint

This recipe can be doubled or adjusted to suit personal tastes. Because crackers don't need to rise, whole wheat flour works well in this recipe, or you could try rye or buckwheat flour instead. You can also substitute fruit juice or water for the wine.

Rosemary Wine Crackers

Bite-You-Back Roasted Edamame

2 teaspoons vegetable oil
2 teaspoons honey
¼ teaspoon wasabi powder*
1 package (10 ounces) shelled edamame, thawed if frozen
   Kosher salt

Available in the Asian section of most supermarkets and in Asian specialty markets.

1. Preheat oven to 375°F. Combine oil, honey and wasabi powder in large bowl; mix well. Add edamame; toss to coat. Spread on baking sheet in single layer.

2. Bake 12 to 15 minutes or until golden brown, stirring once. Immediately remove from baking sheet; sprinkle generously with salt. Cool completely before serving. Store in airtight container. *Makes 4 servings*

Sweet Onion & Pumpkin Seed Focaccia

¼ cup canola oil
2 medium red onions, thinly sliced (about 5 cups)
¼ cup unsalted shelled pumpkin seeds
½ teaspoon dried oregano
¼ teaspoon salt
⅛ teaspoon red pepper flakes
⅛ teaspoon black pepper
1 package (about 14 ounces) refrigerated pizza dough

1. Preheat oven to 400°F. Grease large baking sheet.

2. Heat oil in large skillet over medium-high heat. Add onions; cook 7 minutes or until onions are almost tender, stirring occasionally. Add pumpkin seeds, oregano, salt, red pepper flakes and black pepper; cook and stir over low heat 3 to 5 minutes.

3. Unroll dough on prepared baking sheet; press into 15×10-inch rectangle. Bake 10 minutes.

4. Spread onion mixture evenly over crust. Bake 10 to 14 minutes or until crust is golden and onions are beginning to brown. Let stand 5 minutes before cutting. *Makes 10 servings*

Bite-You-Back Roasted Edamame

Stromboli Sticks

1 package (13.8 ounces) refrigerated pizza crust dough
10 mozzarella cheese sticks
30 thin slices pepperoni
1 jar (1 pound 10 ounces) RAGÚ® OLD WORLD STYLE®
      Pasta Sauce, heated

1. Preheat oven to 425°F. Grease baking sheet; set aside.

2. Roll pizza dough into 13×10-inch rectangle. Cut in half crosswise, then cut each half into 5 strips.

3. Arrange 1 cheese stick on each strip of pizza dough, then top with 3 slices pepperoni. Fold edges over, sealing tightly.

4. Arrange stromboli sticks on prepared baking sheet, seam side down. Bake 15 minutes or until golden. Serve with Pasta Sauce, heated, for dipping.

Makes 10 sticks

Beef & Roasted Pepper Crostini

¾ pound thinly sliced deli roast beef
3 tablespoons olive oil
2 large cloves garlic, crushed
2 loaves (8 ounces each) French bread (about 2½-inch diameter),
      cut into ½-inch-thick slices
1 jar (12 ounces) roasted red peppers, rinsed, drained, chopped
2 cups shredded Italian cheese blend

1. Heat oven to 450°F. In 1-cup glass measure, combine oil and garlic; microwave on HIGH 30 seconds. Lightly brush top side of each bread slice with oil mixture; arrange on 2 baking sheets. Bake in 450°F oven 6 to 8 minutes or until light golden brown.

2. Layer equal amounts of beef, red peppers and cheese over toasted bread. Return to oven; bake an additional 2 to 4 minutes or until cheese is melted. Serve immediately.

Makes about 36 appetizers

Tip: Bread may be toasted ahead of time; store in airtight container.

Prep and Cook Time: 30 minutes

Favorite recipe from **The Beef Checkoff**

Stromboli Sticks

Citrus-Marinated Olives

1 cup (about 8 ounces) large green olives, drained
1 cup kalamata olives, rinsed and drained
⅓ cup extra-virgin olive oil
1 tablespoon grated orange peel
¼ cup orange juice
3 tablespoons sherry vinegar or red wine vinegar
1 tablespoon grated lemon peel
2 tablespoons lemon juice
½ teaspoon ground cumin
¼ teaspoon red pepper flakes

Combine all ingredients in medium glass bowl. Let stand overnight at room temperature; refrigerate for up to two weeks.   *Makes 2 cups olives*

Polenta Triangles

3 cups cold water
1 cup yellow cornmeal
1 envelope LIPTON® RECIPE SECRETS® Golden Onion or
    Onion Soup Mix
1 can (4 ounces) mild chopped green chilies, drained
½ cup thawed frozen or drained canned whole kernel corn
⅓ cup finely chopped roasted red peppers
½ cup shredded sharp Cheddar cheese (about 2 ounces)

1. In 3-quart saucepan, bring water to a boil over high heat. With wire whisk, stir in cornmeal, then soup mix. Reduce heat to low and simmer uncovered, stirring constantly, 25 minutes or until thickened. Stir in chilies, corn and roasted red peppers.

2. Spread into lightly greased 9-inch square baking pan; sprinkle with cheese. Let stand 20 minutes or until firm; cut into triangles. Serve at room temperature or heat in oven at 350°F for 5 minutes or until warm.

Makes about 24 triangles

Citrus-Marinated Olives

Toasted Ravioli with Fresh Tomato-Basil Salsa

1 package (about 9 ounces) refrigerated cheese ravioli
¾ cup plain dry bread crumbs
2 tablespoons grated Parmesan cheese
1 teaspoon dried basil
1 teaspoon dried oregano
¼ teaspoon black pepper
2 egg whites
Fresh Tomato-Basil Salsa (recipe follows)

1. Cook ravioli according to package directions. Rinse under cold running water until cool; drain well.

2. Preheat oven to 375°F. Spray nonstick baking sheet with olive oil cooking spray.

3. Combine bread crumbs, cheese, basil, oregano and pepper in medium bowl. Beat egg whites lightly in shallow dish. Add ravioli to egg whites; toss lightly to coat. Transfer ravioli, a few at a time, to bread crumb mixture; toss to coat evenly. Arrange on prepared baking sheet; spray tops of ravioli with cooking spray.

4. Bake 12 to 14 minutes or until crisp. Meanwhile, prepare Fresh Tomato-Basil Salsa; serve with ravioli for dipping.   *Makes 8 servings*

Fresh Tomato-Basil Salsa: Combine 1 pound fresh tomatoes, peeled and seeded, ½ cup loosely packed fresh basil leaves, ¼ small onion, 1 teaspoon red wine vinegar and ¼ teaspoon salt in food processor. Process until finely chopped but not smooth.

Toasted Ravioli with Fresh Tomato-Basil Salsa

Pretzel Dippers

⅓ cup spicy brown mustard
3 tablespoons whipped butter
2 tablespoons mayonnaise
1 package frozen soft pretzels (6 pretzels)
24 thin slices salami, cut into halves
10 ounces Swiss cheese, cut into scant ½-inch cubes

1. Whisk mustard, butter and mayonnaise in small bowl until well blended.

2. Dampen pretzels with water and sprinkle with salt from package according to package directions. Microwave 2 minutes or until pretzels are warm.

3. Cut each pretzel into 8 pieces. Wrap half slice of salami around each pretzel piece; top with cheese cube and secure with toothpick. Serve with mustard sauce for dipping.   *Makes 48 pieces*

Merry Crisps

1 cup all-purpose flour
½ teaspoon baking powder
½ teaspoon paprika
¼ teaspoon salt
⅓ cup plus 1 tablespoon water, divided
3 tablespoons vegetable oil
1 egg white
    Assorted toppings such as seasoned salt, dried basil or poppy seeds

1. Combine flour, baking powder, paprika and salt in medium bowl. Stir in ⅓ cup water and oil to form smooth dough; cover and refrigerate 10 to 15 minutes.

2. Preheat oven to 400°F. Grease baking sheets. Roll out dough on floured surface to 14×12-inch rectangle. Cut out dough using 1- to 1½-inch holiday cookie cutters. Gather and reroll scraps; make additional cutouts. Place on prepared baking sheets.

3. Combine egg white and remaining 1 tablespoon water; brush over cutouts. Sprinkle with desired toppings.

4. Bake 6 to 8 minutes or until edges begin to brown. Remove to wire racks to cool completely.   *Makes 7½ dozen crackers*

Pretzel Dippers

Thai Pizza

1 package JENNIE-O TURKEY STORE® Breast Strips
2 teaspoons bottled or fresh minced ginger
2 teaspoons bottled or fresh minced garlic
¼ teaspoon crushed red pepper flakes
   Cooking spray
¼ cup hoisin or stir-fry sauce
1 large (12-inch) prepared pizza crust
⅓ cup thinly sliced green onions
½ teaspoon finely grated lime peel
⅓ cup coarsely chopped roasted peanuts
2 tablespoons chopped cilantro or basil

Heat oven to 450°F. Toss turkey strips with ginger, garlic and pepper flakes. Coat large nonstick skillet with cooking spray; heat over medium-high heat. Add turkey; stir-fry 2 minutes. Add hoisin sauce; stir-fry 2 minutes. Place pizza crust on large cookie sheet. Spread mixture evenly over pizza crust; sprinkle with green onions and lime peel. Bake 8 to 10 minutes or until crust is golden brown and hot. Sprinkle with peanuts and cilantro. Cut into wedges. *Makes 12 appetizer servings*

Pita Cheese Straws

3 pita bread rounds (6 inches)
2 tablespoons butter, melted
1 clove garlic, pressed
1 teaspoon Italian seasoning
¼ cup grated Parmesan cheese
   French onion dip

1. Preheat oven to 350°F. Split pitas in half. Combine butter, garlic and Italian seasoning in small bowl.

2. Brush tops of pitas with butter mixture; sprinkle with Parmesan. Cut into ½-inch strips with pizza cutter. Arrange strips in single layer on ungreased baking sheet.

3. Bake 8 to 10 minutes or until edges are deep golden brown. Serve with dip. *Makes 6 servings*

Thai Pizza

Sweet & Spicy Beer Nuts

2 cups pecan halves
2 teaspoons salt
2 teaspoons chili powder
2 teaspoons olive oil
½ teaspoon ground cumin
¼ teaspoon ground red pepper
½ cup sugar
½ cup beer

1. Preheat oven to 350°F. Line baking sheet with foil.

2. Mix pecans, salt, chili powder, olive oil, cumin and red pepper in small bowl. Spread on prepared baking sheet. Bake 10 minutes or until nuts are fragrant. Cool on baking sheet on wire rack.

3. Combine sugar and beer in small saucepan. Heat over medium-high heat until mixture registers 250°F on candy thermometer. Remove from heat; carefully stir in nuts and any loose spices. Spread sugared nuts on foil-lined baking sheet, separating clusters. Cool; break up any large pieces before serving. *Makes 3 cups nuts*

Thai Chicken Skewers

¼ cup creamy peanut butter
2 tablespoons finely chopped onion
2 tablespoons finely chopped parsley
2 tablespoons fresh lemon juice
1½ teaspoons soy sauce
1 clove garlic, finely chopped
1 teaspoon Original TABASCO® brand Pepper Sauce
½ teaspoon ground coriander
1 pound boneless, skinless chicken breasts, cut into 1-inch pieces
Wooden skewers

Combine all ingredients except chicken and skewers in medium bowl. Add chicken; toss to coat. Cover and refrigerate 6 to 8 hours or overnight.

Preheat broiler or grill. Thread marinated chicken on skewers. Broil or grill 6 to 8 minutes, turning frequently. (Do not overcook.) Serve warm on skewers. *Makes 30 to 35 pieces*

Sweet & Spicy Beer Nuts

Super Salami Twists

1 egg, slightly beaten
1 tablespoon milk
1 cup finely chopped hard salami (about 4 ounces)
2 tablespoons yellow cornmeal
1 teaspoon Italian seasoning
1 package (11 ounces) refrigerated breadstick dough
¾ cup marinara sauce, heated

1. Preheat oven to 375°F. Line baking sheet with foil or parchment paper.

2. Beat egg and milk in shallow dish until well blended. Combine salami, cornmeal and Italian seasoning in separate shallow dish.

3. Unroll breadstick dough; separate into 12 pieces along perforations. Roll each dough piece in egg mixture, then in salami mixture, gently pressing salami into dough. Twist each piece of dough twice and place on prepared baking sheet.

4. Bake 13 to 15 minutes or until golden brown. Remove to wire rack; cool 5 minutes. Serve warm with marinara sauce for dipping.

Makes 12 twists

Prep Time: 10 minutes
Bake Time: 13 minutes

Italian Pita Chips

½ cup (1 stick) butter, melted
1 packet Italian dressing mix
4 pita bread rounds, split in half

1. Preheat oven to 300°F. Spray baking sheet with nonstick cooking spray.

2. Combine butter and dressing mix in small bowl. Brush mixture over tops of pitas and place on prepared baking sheet. Bake about 20 minutes or until crisp.

3. Carefully break into pieces. Serve with your favorite dip or spread.

Makes 4 servings

Super Salami Twists

Paprika-Spiced Almonds

1 cup whole blanched almonds
¾ teaspoon olive oil
¼ teaspoon coarse salt
¼ teaspoon smoked paprika or paprika

1. Preheat oven to 375°F. Spread almonds in single layer in shallow baking pan. Bake 8 to 10 minutes or until almonds are lightly browned. Transfer to bowl; cool 5 to 10 minutes.

2. Toss almonds with oil until completely coated. Sprinkle with salt and paprika; toss again. *Makes about 8 servings*

Tip: For the best flavor, serve these almonds the day they are made.

Crisp Tortellini Bites

½ cup plain dry bread crumbs
¼ cup grated Parmesan cheese
2 teaspoons HERB-OX® chicken flavored bouillon
¼ teaspoon garlic powder
½ cup sour cream
2 tablespoons milk
1 (9-ounce) package refrigerated cheese-filled tortellini
Warm pizza sauce or marinara sauce, for dipping

Heat oven to 400°F. In small bowl, combine bread crumbs, Parmesan cheese, bouillon and garlic powder. In another small bowl, combine sour cream and milk. Dip tortellini in sour cream mixture, then in bread crumbs; coat evenly. Place tortellini on baking sheet. Bake 10 to 12 minutes or until crisp and golden brown, turning once. Serve immediately with warm pizza or marinara sauce. *Makes 8 servings*

Tip: The bouillon mixture also makes a great coating for chicken fingers or mild fish.

Paprika-Spiced Almonds

Cheese Twists

1 cup all-purpose flour
½ teaspoon baking soda
½ teaspoon salt
½ teaspoon dry mustard
⅛ teaspoon ground red pepper
¾ cup grated Parmesan cheese, divided
½ cup (1 stick) butter, softened
3 egg yolks
2 teaspoons water
1 egg white, lightly beaten
1 tablespoon sesame seeds (optional)

1. Preheat oven to 400°F. Grease 2 baking sheets.

2. Combine flour, baking soda, salt, mustard and red pepper in large bowl. Reserve 1 tablespoon Parmesan; stir remaining Parmesan into flour mixture. Cut in butter with pastry blender or 2 knives until mixture resembles fine crumbs. Add egg yolks and water; mix until dough forms. Shape into disc; wrap tightly in plastic wrap. Refrigerate 2 hours or until firm.

3. Roll out dough on lightly floured surface into 12-inch square (about ⅛ inch thick). Brush lightly with egg white; sprinkle with remaining 1 tablespoon Parmesan and sesame seeds, if desired. Cut dough in half. Cut each half crosswise into ¼-inch strips. Twist 2 strips together. Repeat with remaining strips. Place twists 1 inch apart on prepared baking sheets.

4. Bake 6 to 8 minutes or until light golden brown. Remove to wire racks to cool completely. Store in airtight container. *Makes about 48 twists*

Acknowledgments

The publisher would like to thank the companies and organizations listed below for the use of their recipes and photographs in this publication.

ACH Food Companies, Inc.

Allens®

Alouette® Spreadable Cheese, Alouette® Baby Brie®, Alouette® Crème Spreadable, Chavrie®, Saladena®

Courtesy of The Beef Checkoff

Bob Evans®

Cabot® Creamery Cooperative

Del Monte Corporation

Dole Food Company, Inc.

The Hershey Company

Hillshire Farm®

Holland House®

Hormel Foods, LLC

Jennie-O Turkey Store, LLC

McIlhenny Company (TABASCO® brand Pepper Sauce)

National Pork Board

Nestlé USA

Newman's Own, Inc.®

Ortega®, A Division of B&G Foods, Inc.

Pacific Northwest Canned Pear Service

Reckitt Benckiser Inc.

Sargento® Foods Inc.

Sun•Maid® Growers of California

Unilever

Walnut Marketing Board

Wisconsin Milk Marketing Board

Index

156

Index

Index

Metric Conversion Chart

VOLUME
MEASUREMENTS (dry)

$^1/_8$ teaspoon = 0.5 mL
$^1/_4$ teaspoon = 1 mL
$^1/_2$ teaspoon = 2 mL
$^3/_4$ teaspoon = 4 mL
1 teaspoon = 5 mL
1 tablespoon = 15 mL
2 tablespoons = 30 mL
$^1/_4$ cup = 60 mL
$^1/_3$ cup = 75 mL
$^1/_2$ cup = 125 mL
$^2/_3$ cup = 150 mL
$^3/_4$ cup = 175 mL
1 cup = 250 mL
2 cups = 1 pint = 500 mL
3 cups = 750 mL
4 cups = 1 quart = 1 L

VOLUME MEASUREMENTS (fluid)

1 fluid ounce (2 tablespoons) = 30 mL
4 fluid ounces ($^1/_2$ cup) = 125 mL
8 fluid ounces (1 cup) = 250 mL
12 fluid ounces (1$^1/_2$ cups) = 375 mL
16 fluid ounces (2 cups) = 500 mL

WEIGHTS (mass)

$^1/_2$ ounce = 15 g
1 ounce = 30 g
3 ounces = 90 g
4 ounces = 120 g
8 ounces = 225 g
10 ounces = 285 g
12 ounces = 360 g
16 ounces = 1 pound = 450 g

DIMENSIONS

$^1/_{16}$ inch = 2 mm
$^1/_8$ inch = 3 mm
$^1/_4$ inch = 6 mm
$^1/_2$ inch = 1.5 cm
$^3/_4$ inch = 2 cm
1 inch = 2.5 cm

OVEN TEMPERATURES

250°F = 120°C
275°F = 140°C
300°F = 150°C
325°F = 160°C
350°F = 180°C
375°F = 190°C
400°F = 200°C
425°F = 220°C
450°F = 230°C

BAKING PAN SIZES

Utensil	Size in Inches/Quarts	Metric Volume	Size in Centimeters
Baking or	8×8×2	2 L	20×20×5
Cake Pan	9×9×2	2.5 L	23×23×5
(square or	12×8×2	3 L	30×20×5
rectangular)	13×9×2	3.5 L	33×23×5
Loaf Pan	8×4×3	1.5 L	20×10×7
	9×5×3	2 L	23×13×7
Round Layer	8×1½	1.2 L	20×4
Cake Pan	9×1½	1.5 L	23×4
Pie Plate	8×1¼	750 mL	20×3
	9×1¼	1 L	23×3
Baking Dish	1 quart	1 L	—
or Casserole	1½ quart	1.5 L	—
	2 quart	2 L	—